ONLY
BY
GRACE

How I Met the Savoir
and
How He Changed My Life

Bill Lenz

FIRST SILVER THREAD PUBLISHING EDITION,
JANUARY 2019
Silver Thread Publishing is a division of A Silver Thread Pismo Beach CA
www.asilverthread.com
ISBN 978-0-9991794-8-2
Printed in the United States of America

FOREWORD

Only by Grace is an apt title for the story of Bill Lenz's life. It was the phrase with which he regularly signed his correspondence. It summarized the reality by which he lived his life. As a young boy, Bill was loved deeply by parents who knew more than their share of pain and suffering. While he was secure in a loving family environment, Bill was desperately insecure outside the home, where he was mentally and verbally abused. Shy, confused, and socially rejected, he turned to the drug culture at a fairly early age. School work, athletic involvement, and most of all, family life were negatively affected and his despair deepened. At this point in his life, he was introduced to the God of Grace - so called because He is gracious to the helpless and the hurting, generous to the undeserving, and good to the ungrateful. Bill called out to the Lord, who graciously heard his cry, and his life was changed.

Many people contributed to his spiritual life as God graciously brought them into Bill's life, and at the same time, he went out of his way to his "druggy" friends and began to tell them what the Lord had done. Immediately, young people saw the change in Bill and began to respond to his "message." Understandably, because he had grown up with a brother and a sister who were severely handicapped, Bill had a huge heart for the underprivileged, and they began to embrace the gospel of Grace.

A church was born; Bill's latent gifts (gifts of grace) began to blossom - a pastoral heart, a visionary focus, a clear unpretentious gift of communication and compassion for the hurting, and a humble spirit. Local people saw it, they recognized a changed life and flocked to know what had happened to Bill - so he told them. He'd been saved by grace through faith! This is a story of grace!

It is tragic that Bill's life was cut off prematurely, but we take comfort in the fact that the work of grace begun in his teenage years, while incomplete on earth, has been completed in heaven for all eternity by God's grace.

Stuart Briscoe
Telling the Truth Ministries

Only by Grace

But God, being rich in mercy, because of His great love with which He loved us, even when we were dead in our transgressions, made us alive together with Christ.

By grace you have been saved and raised us up with Him, and seated us with Him in the heavenly places in Christ Jesus, so that in the ages to come He might show the surpassing riches of His grace in kindness toward us in Christ Jesus.

For by grace you have been saved through faith; and hat not of yourselves, it is the gift of God; not as a result of works, so that no one may boast. For we are His workmanship, created in Christ Jesus for good works, which God prepared beforehand so that we would walk in them.

Ephesians 2:4-10

NASB

Chapter 1

YOU CAN STAND UP HERE!

Little Chute is a small village tucked along the banks of the Fox River. The Fox runs through a luxurious valley from a large inland lake (Lake Winnebago) to the Bay of Lake Michigan. In March of 1848, forty families set sail from Rotterdam, Holland and after a long journey across the Atlantic and a three-week delay in the Straights of Mackinac, they finally arrived in Green Bay. They continued their voyage in flat boats 25 miles south on the Fox River to settle in La Petite Chute (Little Rapids).

I grew up in this village, only 25 miles from the home of the famous Green Bay Packers. Milwaukee is 100 miles south, and Madison, the state capital, is 100 miles to the southwest. Apart from the Packers, Wisconsin is best known for its cheese and outdoor recreational activities. The state is home to several national forests and many lakes. It's easy to be an outdoor enthusiast, and I was no exception. My life is filled with many stories of fishing, hunting, and great outdoor adventures.

My earliest memories revolve around family; parents who loved each other and wanted to raise a family. Life was simple. Playing outside with my friends and going to the family cottage. Childhood was a funny thing to me. Seems like all the good times and pleasant memories run together, while the difficult and painful ones stand out with greater detail.

When I was four, my mom had a baby right before Christmas. She carried the baby to term, but the umbilical cord wrapped around his neck during birth and he suffocated. His name was Joseph. Two years later, my mom went to the hospital and came home with another baby brother. They named him Bob. I was glad to have a brother.

I had mixed feelings about going to kindergarten. I walked to school every day with my sister, Lois, who was a year older than me, and my best friend Gary. Early in the school year, I learned that my sister would be placed in my class. She was having some problems in first grade, and they wanted her to repeat kindergarten. I was excited that Lois would be in class with me until a few weeks later, when another girl started to make fun of her. She teased about her runny nose and her inability to accomplish simple tasks. A few others joined in. I stood up for her and felt the sting of their unfair treatment. My defense didn't stop this girl; she continued even more and pulled for more attention from others in the class. That was the first time I remembered feeling a profound sense of confusion and shame.

I was surprised at the treatment Lois received. Others didn't seem to like her. I thought she was the greatest. She was my sister and my playmate, and I had so much fun with her. It never occurred to me that someone else could feel differently about her. I never noticed the things they were pointing out about her and laughing at. I thought, "What is wrong with Lois that makes her unusual or abnormal? Is there something wrong with me, too? Will the other kids not like me because they don't like her?" I didn't know what to do with these thoughts - it just added to my confusion.

Lois continued to face challenges in school and was not learning like the rest of the class. My mom told me they were pulling her out of school a few days for some special testing. Lois seemed fine to me, so I couldn't figure out what the fuss was about. What I knew is that my parents loved me and her, and if that's what they thought needed to be done, it was fine with me. Several weeks later, my mom explained that Lois would probably have to go to a special school. I hated hearing that news. I was confused but also very sad. I felt like I was losing a close friend. I didn't want her to go to a different school; I wanted her to go to my school! I would take care of her! I would watch out for her! I could help her learn! I had so many questions and so many new feelings. My parents tried to comfort and assure me and help me understand. But I wanted to blame someone. "If the kids in my class hadn't treated her so bad, she would still be in my classroom!" I wondered if there was something wrong or weird about our family. I didn't want to think about it, so I tried to put it out of my mind.

Lois was eventually placed in a school for handicapped children, specifically designed to meet the needs of kids who learn at different levels. We later found out that she was mentally retarded, possibly from brain damage which occurred during her birth. My mom had been in labor for several days with Lois, and the doctors said the trauma might cause side effects.

I was cute in my early school years (so Mother told me) and people gravitated toward me; Not toward Lois. I remember the attention. I remember liking it. I was quite inquisitive, free-spirited and playful. But as I got older and encountered people's reactions to Lois....the staring, pointing, and laughter, I started to shut down. I felt a deep love and loyalty to my sister, yet a growing sense of shame of being seen with her in public. I was often torn between defending and fighting, and just running and hiding.

My grandma Lenz ran a grocery store called *Lenz's Keenway*. My dad and my Uncle Dick worked there. I helped out pretty regularly. I filled the pop machine and occasionally earned enough money for candy. Sometimes, I helped Dad stock shelves or unload a truck when a food order came in. Eventually, Dad went to work for the food distribution company that supplied our store. When larger grocery stores started opening, it forced our little Keenway out of business.

My Grandpa Lenz, who I am named after, worked in a paper mill on the Fox River. Paper was the mainstay industry of the Fox River Valley and many cities were built around them. When grandpa was 18, he was working on a paper machine when some paper entered the roller crooked. When he reached to straighten it, his hand got caught in the roller. He reached with his other hand to try to get it out, and that hand was caught as well. He lost both arms that day just past the elbow. My grandpa was fitted with artificial arms, and he learned to use them well. After the accident, he became a mail carrier at the mill.

I have vivid pictures in my mind of him holding a cane pole with his artificial limbs to catch perch and keeping up with the rest of us. He and grandma lived next door, so in my teen years, I'd go over there daily to help him get his harnesses and artificial arms on. I also helped my grandma who was in a wheelchair and needed help with the open sores she had on her legs.

I had a lot of friends and we played hard...games, hanging out in a wooded ravine and creek and shooting pellet guns and building forts. The ravine became the best sledding spot in the winter. We called it Suicide Hill because of the rough terrain.

The best thing of all was to be at the family cottage. My father's parents built a small cottage on Lake Poygan shortly after the Great Depression. Grandpa paid $100 for the lake lot and used wood scraps from the mill to build it. Nothing fancy, but it was my favorite place to be. There was always so much to do there...swimming, fishing, boating, and playing in the sandbox or live-well tank. But from early on, my dad and grandpa made sure we chipped in with the work. They always told us that having a place like that provided a lot of fun, but also a lot of responsibility. Helping out and working hard became a normal part of life, even though we never liked it. Grandpa always insisted we do the work first. I always tried to have fun first.

When I was ten, I was at the cottage with my best friend, Gary. We boated out in the lake 200 yards from shore. A big storm kicked up out of nowhere. We climbed in the boat to row back to safety, but the wind was strong and blew the air mattress out of the boat. Without thinking, I jumped in to retrieve it. The wind blew it out of my reach each time I got close. The waves were getting bigger. I was getting farther and farther from the boat. I panicked. Gary rowed as hard as he could to get to me and extended an oar, but I couldn't reach it. The waves were pushing the red boat past me, and I swam hard to catch it. As the boat got closer, Gary extended an oar from the back, but every time I reached for it, a wave tossed me and I went under. I already went down twice and inhaled a lot of water. I was certain I was going to drown.

I looked up one more time to try to reach the extended oar and saw Gary jump into the water to help me. He grabbed me and held me up to get some air. I heard him yelling, "Bill, you can stand up here, you can stand up here!"

He didn't know that when he jumped in. He risked his life trying to save mine.

That's a true friend.

Chapter 2

THEN CAME TIM

When I was eight years old, my mother went to the hospital again to have a baby. I stayed with my aunt and uncle. Aunt Eileen explained to me that Mom was suffering complications and that the baby wasn't coming out. She was in labor for several days, and the doctors weren't sure what to do. Finally the baby was born - I had a new brother. I was so excited. Aunt Eileen told me that mom and my brother wouldn't be home for a few weeks because there were some problems and they had to do some tests.

It seemed like forever but they finally came home. My parents explained what happened during the birth, but Tim looked fine to me. He was diagnosed as a quadriplegic. He was like Lois, mentally retarded, but he also had cerebral palsy, scoliosis, and some other things I didn't understand and couldn't pronounce.

As Tim got older, his problems became more evident. He was sick a lot. He had repeated seizures and high temperatures. He screamed in pain, and we would take turns holding him, walking him, and putting cold towels on him to bring the fever down. We'd panic as his temperature would sometimes reach 105 degrees. There were many sleepless nights as we took turns comforting Tim and trying to ease his pain. His arms and legs would stiffen, and his body would tense and freeze during each seizure. We'd rub his back and arms gently and say, "It's okay Timmer, it's okay...you're going to be alright."

After several minutes, he would start to calm down. Often, he'd go from one seizure right into the next, and his eyes would roll and his mouth would twitch. We felt so helpless to make them go away.

My parents took him to one specialist after another. One tried to figure out medications, another determined the type of braces he needed, and yet another would recommend exercises and therapy.

The time came and went when Tim should have learned how to crawl and walk. We questioned whether he ever would develop those basic skills. He had braces to help straighten his crooked legs and feet and a walker that helped him learn how to stand on his legs while supporting himself with his arms. He scooted around the house and seemed to enjoy it.

But he still needed to be carried everywhere and have everything done for him. It consumed mother's time and energy. My dad helped as he could, but he left for work at 2:00 p.m. and didn't get home until after 10:00 p.m. Mom needed help from me and my brother, Bob, especially when dad was at work. We didn't mind. Tim was our brother and we loved him.

Going places as a family was difficult. Tim was in a wheelchair and his handicaps were much more severe and noticeable than were Lois's. I wasn't prepared for the public reaction. He drew a lot of attention and disdain. I was stunned by how people would stare and the comments they made. I loved Tim. He was my brother. He didn't do anything wrong. He didn't ask for this...neither did I or my parents. "Why don't people like him?" I asked myself. Why did their disdain of him affect the way I felt about him? Why did I love to be with him yet feel such shame when I was seen with him? The older I got, the more aware I became of this battle. Every time we would go places with our family or push my brother around the block in his wheelchair, I had to fight the shame.

I started to wonder why God would allow this to happen. Most families didn't have anyone who was handicapped. Why did we have two? It just didn't seem fair. Did we do something wrong to deserve this? Was God punishing us for something we did?

When Timmer was just over two years old, Mom went to the hospital to have another baby. I was scared and wondered if there would be complications again. I was so relieved when I heard that I had a normal, healthy baby brother. They named him Jim. Mom needed a lot of extra help now, with the new baby and still having to provide so much care for Timmer. Lois needed help, too, not nearly as much as Tim, but she needed help getting dressed and with other daily routines.

By the time I was ten, my life consisted of going to school, playing with neighborhood friends, going hunting and fishing with my dad, and helping at home. Lois and I still got along great and played a lot of indoor games. We'd bargain that if I played dolls with her, she'd play pool with me. We played and laughed a lot together. I didn't feel any ambivalence toward Lois or Tim at home. I only felt awkward about them in public. Why did it matter so much what other people thought or said?

Chapter 3

MY DAD, MY FRIEND

From my earliest years, memories of my father are fond ones. He was a gentle man who wasn't afraid to show affection or say, "I love you." I always got a hug and a kiss at night before going to bed. He or my mom would say bedtime prayers with me and tuck me in.

When I was younger, he worked at my grandparents' grocery store, Lenz's Keenway. He always asked me to come over while he was working, either to help him out or just to be with him. He gave me small jobs, and if I did well, he'd give me bigger jobs. One of my favorites was filling the soda machine.

Those were the days when soda came in bottles, and the inside of the caps had faces of different NFL football players. I always got excited to open the machine and check to see how many caps were in there and if there were any players I didn't have yet. I felt pretty important getting the money from the machine and bringing it to my grandmother. Occasionally, my dad would let me stock shelves, and I even helped unload semi trucks when a big food order came in.

When I was seven, my dad took a job at the warehouse of the food supplier that supplied our store. The future of the Keenway wasn't too bright because of a new and bigger grocery store that had opened in town. That's when my dad started working the 2:00 p.m. to 10:00 p.m. shift. We always begged to stay up until he'd come home from work. As we got older, we were allowed to and would often have pizza with him when he got home.

My best memories with my dad were weekends. My mom was consumed with caring for Lois and Tim, so she encouraged my dad to take the boys out on weekends. And that's what he did my whole life growing up. In spring, it would be fishing; in summer, it was the cottage. There was so much to do there. We loved to fish, swim, tube, water ski, take boat rides, catch turtles, dive for clams and build forts. In the fall was rabbit hunting. There's nothing like being out in the woods in October and November listening to a beagle howl and waiting for that rabbit to circle. My dad always had beagles. There was Smokey, Mitsy, Tiny, Becky, Mercury, Thunder and Hunter.

After rabbit hunting would be bow hunting for deer, then gun deer hunting, which would end just in time for ice fishing, which would bring us back to spring fishing again.

We had many good talks on those weekends in the woods or on a lake. All I had to do is say, "Dad, do you remember the time...", and he would take over and tell the story. He remembered hundreds of events with such detail. What a joy to hear him tell and retell the stories of our outdoor adventures. The one that stands out to me was when I was seven, and we went northern pike fishing in early spring. We anchored and threw out a few big minnows with bobbers letting them soak while we would cast. My dad hauled in a beautiful 35 inch northern, and we knew we were in a good spot. Suddenly, his big bobber disappeared, and he told me to grab it.

"But that's your pole, Dad!"

"I know," he said, "but I want you to catch one."

He coached me and told me when to set the hook. I reeled in as hard as I could, and it felt like there was a whale on the other end. It started to come in as I was winding, but all of a sudden, it decided to run, and the reel went spinning and the handle spun backwards and bent my thumb back. I was in pain and handed the pole to my dad. He held it long enough to play it out a bit and for my thumb to recover, then he handed the pole back to me. He coached me until I had it close enough to net. It was a 32 inch northern and looked like a world record to me! My dad was so excited - even more excited than when he caught his, even though his was bigger. I tasted the genuineness of my father's joy for me. I knew he wanted nothing more than to see his son catch a big fish that day. What a thrill it was for me, not just to catch a big fish, but to experience my dad's delight in me and my experience.

He caught another large fish that day, but when we pulled into our driveway at home, he said, "Get mom and show her." Then he said, "call your friends and tell them to come and see." The camera recorded our big catch that day.

I always considered my dad to be one of my best friends. He was easy to talk to and fun to be around. But there was one thing I didn't understand. I'm sure my parents told me that my father was an epileptic, but I had no frame of reference until the first time I saw my dad have a seizure. I was scared and didn't know what to do. His whole body shook, his eyes moved wildly, and his head was jerking all over while he made deep sounds. My mom tried to put his wallet in his mouth to keep him from biting or swallowing his tongue. After a few minutes, which seemed like forever to me, he calmed down and was lying still. Mom assured me he would be alright; he just needed to rest. After he regained consciousness, he didn't remember anything at first. Gradually, he started remembering who we were and what happened just prior to the seizure. He was sore but everything else was fine. I was just glad he was okay.

The first time that I remember my dad had a seizure in public was at church. I was concerned with helping him and making sure he was okay, but I also had a strong awareness that people were watching. It was the same feeling I had with Lois and Tim; torn between loving my dad, yet battling the shame that came with my association with him because of what others would think or say. My friends from the neighborhood didn't seem to be affected by any of this. It didn't matter to them that my sister, brother, and father had these problems. My best friend, Gary, acted like he didn't even notice.

A terrifying time was when my grandpa, my dad, my brother, and I were fishing in a 16 foot fiberglass boat. Suddenly, I heard a pounding noise and the whole boat began to shake. My grandpa yelled, "grab him - don't let him go totally in the water." My dad's head was already over the side of the boat, bobbing in and out of the water. His whole body was so tight, strong, and shaking. We grabbed him and tried to pull him back into the boat. I felt terror inside because it felt like we weren't going to hold him from going over. Gradually, the seizure started to subside, and we were able to get him back into the boat. I don't remember ever being more afraid or feeling so helpless. I was twelve and my brother was only six. When we got back to shore, he slept for a long time. When he woke up, he didn't remember anything that happened, except he felt terrible regret every time he had a seizure.

When I was in eighth grade, I was one of the managers for the basketball team. A lot of my friends were on the team, so being a manager allowed me to be with them. Our team did well that year and played in a championship game. Late in the fourth quarter, I was sitting near the table that kept record of the game and controlled the scoreboard, when suddenly the referees blew their whistles to stop the game. They announced that it appeared someone had a heart attack and asked if there was a doctor in the audience. My friend turned to me and said, "Bill, I think it's your father."

I knew instantly he had a seizure. I felt so helpless. I felt such shame. I wanted to crawl out under the bleachers and disappear. Yet, I felt bad for my father and for my mom who was tending to him with everyone watching.

I didn't ride the bus home after the game. Instead I rode home with a friend and his parents. He talked me into going to Bill's Lunch, a small hamburger joint with foosball and pool tables, where everyone would be hanging out to celebrate the victory. When we walked in, it felt like everyone turned to look at me and got quiet. Then one of my classmates yelled out, "hey Lenz, was that your dad?", as he laughed and simulated having a seizure and falling to the floor.

I immediately turned around and ran out of there and kept on running, not quite sure where I was going.

I ended up laying on the ground in an open field, looking at the stars, crying and asking "why? why? why?"

After what seemed to be hours, I got up and walked home. When I went into the house, my mother hugged me and told me my dad was in the living room feeling terrible. He kept saying, "I'm sorry, I'm so sorry."

I said, "but Dad, you didn't do anything wrong."

He didn't know what happened at Bill's Lunch and I wasn't about to tell him. I know this added to my confusion about life and why God had allowed our family to have three people with handicaps, when most families didn't even have one.

My dad always had time for us. I knew he genuinely cared and loved me. He came to every one of my football games that he possibly could. Several times, he even took off work or switched with someone so he could be at my games.

What a rich heritage I have; so many fond memories stored in my mind of times spent with my father. He was a gentle man who invested so much time and energy into my life. Though I regret he wasn't stronger and wish he'd been more decisive, I am so grateful that I never doubted that my father loved me. I never even wondered about that because I grew up confident that I was loved. I can honestly say that I don't have any painful or bad memories of my dad. They are all good. I know that is pretty unusual.

Charter 4

MY MOM

As I reflect on what my mother was like growing up, my heart leaps with gratitude. She had a heart of gold and had room in her heart for just about anybody, especially if you were hurting. No one could give hugs and affirm like my mom.

She was an incredible cook, and she enjoyed making big meals for the family. Perhaps it came from her parents who ran a Supper Club. I remember going with my mom to Louie's Supper Club when they needed some extra help. She put so much time, energy, and care into the meals. It was one of the ways she showed her love.

Christmas was never a small event at our house. She would go all out to make it special. I have fond memories of spending hours in the kitchen with Mom and my sister and brothers making candy and cookies. She knew how to build up the excitement. We always picked out a tree together as a family, pitched in to decorate it, put up the manger, and recall the Christmas story. When it came to gifts, she always knew what we hoped for. Though the budget was tight, she found a way to make it special.

She was domestic. She never worked outside the home but was content and secure being a wife, mother, and homemaker. Her family was her priority, and none of us ever doubted we were loved. She continually sacrificed for her family. When I think of what it was like for her, day after day, tending to two special needs children, my respect for her grows deeper.

Mom was only twenty when she had Lois and had to face the reality of having a mentally retarded daughter. At twenty-nine, she endured a severe three-day labor with my brother, Tim, who was born a quadriplegic. He lived to be almost twenty years old. He never walked, never talked, and was in diapers until the day he died. Every meal had to be specially made and spoon fed to him. He had to be lifted each time he needed to be moved. As he got older and bigger, the toll on my mother's body was incredible.

My mom never considered putting either of her two handicapped children in an institution. She did whatever it took to keep them home and loved and cared for them well. She never complained or felt sorry for herself. She accepted her difficulties and committed herself to her family. Later in life, people would ask her how she did it. "How did you do it all those years with Lois and Tim?" She jokingly replied, "Lois and Tim were easy, it was Bill and Bob that were difficult to raise."

Mom was a servant. She served well. She loved well. She always put the needs of others above her own. She didn't complain. She found real joy in serving others and in seeing others experience joy. Even with her own load at home, she always found time to cook a meal for another family or make extra cookies to bring to a neighbor. My friends were always welcome in our home. She treated them like they were her own. She always made extra for a meal and invited our friends to stay and eat with us. She was extremely generous.

My parents always had room in their hearts for others. Many times, despite their hardship, they opened their doors and hearts to let others live with them. Dozens found comfort and refuge in their home.

Mom was a "mom's mom". She was a mom to hundreds of people through the years. Most everyone called her "Ma Lenz" because she had that effect on people. There was room in her heart for everyone. She hurt with those who hurt and had incredible compassion.

I recall with great regret the way I treated my mother during my rebellious years. I dishonored her and verbally abused her, often telling her "I hate you!" She was strong enough to contend with me and challenge my decisions. Much of the confusion, anger, and hatred I had for myself and my life came out against her. The more I got involved with drugs, the more out of control I became, and she didn't know what to do with me.

I fought with her the most when my dad was at work. I cursed her out, spit on her, pushed her, told her I wished she was dead and that I hated her. I'm not sure why I spewed the poison inside of me onto her; perhaps deep down I knew her love for me would never change and I was secure in that.

At times, in desperation, she called her brother to come over to try to settle me down. Uncle Jerry was an ex-marine and a strong, 6'4" brick-house. When I knew he was on his way, I'd lock myself in the bathroom and promise to be good to mom until he left. Dad talked to me about how I treated her but had no success.

Near the end of my junior year in high school, I partied all night with friends and got really stoned. Mom was waiting up for me at 1:30 a.m. I saw compassion and concern in her eyes when she asked me where I was and what I was doing. I told her it was none of her (expletive) business, pushed her, and went into the bathroom to look at my red eyes.

She followed me in there and said, "you have a sister who doesn't have a good mind and a brother who doesn't have a good mind...how can you ruin the good mind that you have? You know that these drugs are destroying you."

I replied in anger. "It's my life and I can do whatever I want - leave me alone! Get out of my life!"

She became silent, but as I turned to leave, I saw tears streaming down her face. With such compassion she said, "I hate what you're doing, but I want you to know I will always, always love you."

I rushed out to my basement bedroom, turned on some music, and tried not to think about what had just happened. I kept hearing her words in my heart......I will always, always love you...... For many months those words melted me but also disrupted me. I didn't want to think about it.

Later, after I had quit the drugs, and everything I was running from met me with full force, I became depressed and spent hours in my room crying and beating the walls. Mom heard me wailing in the basement and came down to try to console me. She didn't know what to do or say to help me, but I knew she cared. Sometimes, she would just come down and tell me she loved me and hugged me and encouraged me. Dad joined her when he was home. The tenderness of their care meant so much. They offered to take me to a counselor. They affirmed me. They wanted to help me get through that time. Their love kept me going.

Mom never gave up on me. At my worst, she was still there for me. She persevered. She endured. She didn't quit, even when I pushed her away and hurt her deeply. She sometimes got angry and frustrated and let me have it, but I knew I had it coming. She had the courage to fight with me and for me - she was a warrior.

Chapter 5

MY ADOLESCENT YEARS

I did okay in school. Nothing exceptional, but I learned well and was a B student. One of the things I excelled at was spelling. In sixth grade, I was selected to be on a spelling team that was going to compete with other schools. In a practice run, I misspelled a pretty easy word. The teacher questioned, in front of the whole class, whether I should go with the team for the competition if I couldn't even spell such an easy word. I felt terrible. After class, a girl classmate came up to me and said, "It must run in the family."

I replied, "What do you mean, it must run in the family?"

She responded, "You know, your sister . . . retardation." That left me more confused and perplexed than hurt. Is there something to this, I wondered?

Most of my extracurricular activities involved the outdoors. I looked forward to high school so I could play football. In seventh grade, many of the friends I hung with played basketball and went out for the team. I went out, not because I liked basketball or thought I was good at it, but because my friends did. A slew of kids got cut from the team and I was one of them. In part to be with my friends and in part to help out, I became a manager of the team. Every good team needs a good manager, my dad would tell me. I was manager for the seventh and eighth grade teams, and my parents would come to every game they could. My parents wanted to support me and my role on the team. That meant a lot to me.

I was short and polite people would call me husky. Others used words like stocky, or built to play football, or fat. It was probably only said to me a few times, but it stands out in my mind like it was said daily by many. "Fatty, fatty, 2x4, can't fit through the kitchen door." Why did those words have such power to affect me? One time a kid called me "Billy Bumps." He was referring to my breasts, which appeared bigger than most, I guess. He said I had more than most girls and should consider wearing a bra. After that, whenever I was in a public place, I would never take my shirt off. When swimming, I would cross my arms and put my hands on my shoulders to cover my chest. I became very self-conscious.

In eighth grade, I applied to be a patrol boy. A patrol boy would get a white belt to put on while manning a crossing area when students left school. This was before paid crossing guards became the custom. After a week, I was made a lieutenant. There was one captain, and he got a blue badge, and two lieutenants who got red badges. I was so proud to be a lieutenant and have a red badge. They put me on the main corner, where most kids passed when school was dismissed.

I was standing on my corner my first day excited and anticipating the kids coming. The bell rang and out they came. As they neared, I looked and noticed a car coming. I stretched out my arms to signify they needed to stop.

One of my classmates yelled out, "Lenz, you're so fat you don't even need to put out your arms!" Many of the other kids there laughed, and I laughed. After everyone was gone, I ran home and went to my room, put my head under my pillow and cried a long time. I didn't want to be a patrol boy anymore, and I didn't want to go back to school. But, of course, I did.

I still loved my family but was so tired of people staring and pointing and laughing and making comments. It was easier to avoid them and escape into a make-believe world of ecstasy, created by the illusions brought on by drugs and other forms of escapism.

GO TO HELL

Big, bold, yellow letters on a black basement bedroom wall-- Go to hell! It was the first thing you saw when you walked into my room. As a sophomore in high school, I hated life and hated myself.

Confused, angry, and looking for relief, I started drinking in 7th grade. I started off slow and gradually picked up the pace. A few of us knew some upper classmen who were old enough to get it for us whenever we wanted. By 8th grade, we were drinking once or twice a week, mostly on weekends. It made us feel mature to do something only adults were allowed to do. For me, it became a way to escape....to feel good even if only for a few hours.

I was thirteen years old when I noticed a shift occurring inside of me. I was abandoning my loyalties to my family and finding security and identity with friends. I was on the run, not even sure what I was running from or what I was looking for; but I felt a sense of desperation growing rapidly inside of me. I didn't want to hurt anymore and was pretty open to trying anything that would help take away the pain.

Sometime in my freshman year of high school, I met new friends who introduced me to marijuana. The first time I tried it, I coughed and gagged. It was a miserable experience. But I tried it again a few days later in the attic of a friend's garage, and the experience was different. It was much milder than what I tried before and within a matter of minutes, I had a sensation that was euphoric. I had never felt that way before. I thought, "how could this be wrong when it feels so good?" From that time on, there was no stopping. I wanted to get high every chance I could.

I did whatever I could to escape the painful and unpleasant realities of my life. Drugs, alcohol, girls, music, parties...whatever it took to feel good. High school is mostly a blur. School was something that happened in between my drug use and parties. My friends and I would smoke a few joints almost every morning before school, get reignited during our lunch break and catch a few tokes on the way home from school. Most evenings I spent with a few buddies driving around listening to The Who or REO Speedwagon and passing the pipe. Occasionally, we'd stop in at a party or find some other friends to hang with. During the summer, the big hangout for the druggies was in a wooded area on the Fox River we called The Islands. We'd have campfires and get high together and exchange drugs and other paraphernalia.

By the time I was a junior in high school, my drug involvement turned me into a quiet, reclusive, detached zombie. One of my nicknames became Billy Burnout. There were times I couldn't carry on a conversation with another person. Often, I felt paralyzed not knowing what to say. I'd go for days without talking to anyone and would just shrug my shoulders if someone asked me a question. I felt dead inside, and drugs helped to keep me numb.

DEALER BILL

To support my habit, I began dealing drugs out of my basement bedroom. At first, my parents just thought I had new friends coming over. When they started asking about it, I decided to have just a few designated people do the pick-ups, or I would meet people at a neutral place to make the exchange. I realized soon there was some real money to be made in dealing. I sold enough to completely support my use without cost to me. Because the money was there, I experimented with a few other types of drugs. I dabbled with speed and tried a few milder forms of acid. I didn't like what acid did to me or what I saw it doing to others who were in it much deeper than I was. So, I steered clear of acid and would do speed occasionally to pick me up when I was feeling depressed. Mostly I smoked pot.

I didn't see it, but the marijuana was taking its toll on me. During my junior year, I lived from one high to the next. There was hardly a day the entire school year that I wasn't stoned. How I managed to pull off a B average and letter on the football team is a mystery. I became more and more isolated from my family and from the world. I was going numb. I had no hope. Frustration and anger levels were rising in me, but I had no idea why or what to do with it. So, I kept on the same road - pot, isolation, numbness.

A SWITCH

I was getting in trouble at school treating the teachers like I did my mom - with disdain and disrespect. At the beginning of my senior year, I tried switching from my druggie friends to the drinking crowd. I knew that drugs were taking a toll on me. I knew I was going nowhere. I had to change. Drinking, especially in Wisconsin, was more socially acceptable. I thought it was a step in the right direction.

I was at a party and had a lot to drink...beer mostly, some wine. I borrowed a friend's car to stop in at a different party across town. On the way there, I got pulled over for speeding and was brought down to the police station for drinking and driving. The officer who questioned me was known for despising druggies. He knew I was a druggie, so he started interrogating me. I refused to cooperate. He got mad.

"I'm going to kill you," I said.

He threw me his pistol and said, "Why don't you do it now?"

"I'd have more pleasure killing you when you least expect it," I said.

He exploded and attacked me. He started swinging, and I responded in self-defense. He was out of control. I yelled for help. It took several officers to get him off me and calm him down. I remember feeling such hatred for him and wishing I could kill a man like that.

Shortly after that incident, I realized more clearly my life was headed nowhere. I tried to quit drugs, went back to the church where I grew up, and found a girlfriend who was supportive. She tried to help me. Being numb for so long masked the confusion and pain, so thawing out unleashed incredible feelings of pain, helplessness, and hopelessness that made me want to run back to drugs. I gave in sometimes. Drinking helped but only until I sobered up.

The more I thawed out, the more overwhelmed I was with the deep feelings I had stuffed for years. I hated everything about my life and wanted to die. I was so miserable. I felt like there was no hope for ever getting out of this prison. I assumed that if I stopped doing drugs and tried to help other people, I would feel better. But the more sober I got, the worse I felt. I didn't have a clue what to do.

One day near the end of my senior year, I was walking home from school alone, which was rare. Questions like, *Who are you? Why are you here? Why is man on this earth?* and *Where are you going?* invaded my mind. I couldn't think about anything else. I tried to not think about them, but they kept reappearing. I'd go out with friends at night, come in late, go to my room and listen to Jimmy Hendrix or Janice Joplin or REO. When the music would end, I'd lie in my bed wide awake in the stillness of the early morning. Those questions would bombard me.

I knew there had to be something more. I knew I needed answers to those gnawing questions. I began to search. I began to try to reform myself. I tried so hard to stop doing bad things and start doing more good things. It felt like my wheels were spinning, but I was getting nowhere.

I felt powerless to change anything...I didn't know how to help myself and no one else could help me either. I wanted so badly to die.

"God, why aren't you doing anything? You could snap your fingers and make me feel better! Why don't you do something? Why is life so unfair? Why can't I do anything about it?"

"Please, God, let me die."

The harder I tried to change and get my life together, the worse things got, or at least the worse they felt. Now that I wasn't using regularly, I started to feel and face some of the things I had been running from so much of my life. I never cried so much in my life. I had played football the first three years of high school, but I had decided not to go out as a senior. The assistant coach, Bud, showed up at my door to talk to me about why I wasn't going out. He said I was a good ballplayer, and the team needed me, and I needed the team. He spent a lot of time trying to convince me to go out. Upon his persuasion, I did and I'm glad he talked me into it. Our team went 8-0 that season, and we were rated #1 in the state by the Associated Press for schools our size.

That assistant coach was also the high school guidance counselor. Because of his encouragement and friendship as a coach, I felt comfortable talking to him about personal things as my guidance counselor. There were a few times in my senior year that I thought I was going to crack and ended up in his office. He demonstrated genuine caring and would listen intently and give good advice. On several occasions, he mentioned Jesus and turning to Him and asking Him for help. I didn't understand what he was talking about, but I'm sure there were seeds planted. I found out years later that he was a Christian and would pray regularly for me.

AFTER HIGH SCHOOL

I graduated from high school. That summer, I went to a Department of Natural Resources Conservation Camp. The camp was several months long and was a good experience for me. We worked with the DNR in different tasks of forestry, trimming and taking down trees, and putting in trails in State Parks.

I wondered a lot that summer at camp about my life and where it was headed. I was pretty much out of the woods with drugs, still dabbled a lot with alcohol, but still didn't have a clue about my identity . . . who I was or where I was going with my life? I had entertained the thought of going to college for forestry. I was so confused and empty.

I got back from forestry camp in August of 1975. I had also investigated branches of the military. The one most appealing to me was the United States Coast Guard. It looked attractive to me because I grew up with boats and motors and being on the water. To get some training and be on a boat for four years seemed appealing to me. I enlisted in the Coast Guard and scheduled to leave six months later. I had no clue what I was getting into.

Chapter 6

THE WEEKEND THAT
CHANGED MY LIFE

It was the first week in September 1975. I knew I was going into the Coast Guard but was still very confused about who I was and what my life was about. I was working at EZ-Glide assembling fiberglass garage doors but confusion, frustration, hopelessness still reigned in my life. I felt I was at the end of my rope and decided I needed to get away. I asked my mother to bring me up to my grandparents' cottage and leave me up there for three days. I knew if I took my own vehicle that when nighttime would come, I'd go find a party or a bar, and I didn't want to do that. She conceded and drove me up there. Just 40 minutes from home,

53

on the shore of Lake Poygan, sits an old cottage built by my grandfather and a few of his sons and friends. He was one of the original landowners on that lake and only paid $100 for the lot.

When my mother dropped me off, she handed me a Bible someone had given me ten months earlier. I had been a student helper as a junior for a seventh-grade parochial school teacher. On his bookshelf, he had several copies of *The Way Living Bible*. As I paged through with interest, he offered to give me one. I took it but hadn't touched it since. Now, my mother is handing it to me and encourages me to read it, if I get a chance. "Sure, Mom – thanks!"

She left, and I was on my own. I went out fishing, came in and cleaned up some fish and fried some for lunch. I did some clean-up, fix-up work around the cottage. Time was going very slowly. I picked up that Bible and noticed in the front it had an introduction and some questions. There were questions like, *Are you lonely? Are you hurting? Are you confused?*

After the questions, there was a small list of Bible verse references to look up. I thought, "Shoot, I'm all these things; confused, hurting, lonely, depressed."

So, I started to look up the references, and I was amazed at what I was reading. It made such sense, and it was so relative to what I was thinking and feeling. I could hardly believe how much I related to what I was reading. For some reason, I didn't think anything in that Book related to me personally. I always viewed it as a holy book, with a bunch of rules in it, and things God didn't want us to do, and what happened to people who didn't do what was right. I was stunned.

The question that grabbed me the most was something about, *How to get right with God.* I wanted so badly to change and had been trying for over a year to change, and felt I wasn't really getting anywhere. I felt worse now than I did when I was stoned all the time. So, I looked up the reference, and it was John, chapter 3. I read it slowly. I read about this guy named Nicodemus coming to Jesus at night to ask Him some questions. He started by noting that no one could do the things that Jesus was doing unless God was with Him.

In response to that Jesus said, "Truly, truly I say to you, unless a man is born again, he cannot see the Kingdom of Heaven." That confused Nicodemus a bit, and he asked how someone who is old can go back into his mother's womb and be born again. Jesus then distinguished between the natural birth and a spiritual birth. Jesus then reiterated two more times that unless a man is born again, he will not enter the Kingdom of Heaven (John 3:5-7).

As I read, I was amazed. I had never read this before and had never heard about this before. I felt great because I sensed I was on to something here. I kept reading the other things Jesus said to Nicodemus. I loved what I was reading. I kept reading, thinking it would explain how to be born again. It didn't explain it, but I knew there were answers in what I was reading.

That evening, after having a bite to eat, I turned on the TV and sat on the couch with a Coke. As the TV focused in, Billy Graham was on the screen. I knew briefly who he was because my grandfather would occasionally listen to him on the radio and have me listen. He always had it so loud I never understood what was being said.

I got up to turn the set off, and as I was walking towards the TV, he pointed and said something like, "And you, watching television, listen to what I have to say."

It scared me. I was paranoid. I thought, "Uh-oh, he knows I'm here . . . I'm busted."

Then, he said something like Matthew 24, "Jesus is knocking at your door," and made some reference to being born again.

I was stunned. I couldn't believe that what I had read earlier in the day in the Bible about being born again, that now this guy was going to talk about it and explain it. I sat down and listened intently and hung on every word. He very simply and clearly explained why Jesus came, and why He died. He described how one can have a personal relationship with Jesus Christ and the difference between knowing about someone and actually knowing them personally. He illustrated by saying, "There is a door on every person's heart. Jesus is on the outside knocking on the door. There is no handle or knob on the outside but only on the inside." He said, "Many of you know about Jesus, and maybe even pray and talk to Him, through the door." He said, "You may be a good person and go to church, but that doesn't make you a Christian. It's not until you open the door of your heart, and invite Christ to come in, and ask Him to be your Savior and Lord, that you become a Christian." He quoted John 1:12, "To as many as received Christ, to them He gave the power to become the sons of God." He explained how big of a decision this was but how easy it was. He said, "You must surrender control of your life to the Lordship of Christ, and when you do, your life will never be the same."

When he finished speaking, he invited those at the stadium who wanted to receive Christ to come forward. I watched as hundreds, if not thousands, of people streamed down the aisles to the front. Then, he put his head down and prayed. After a short time, he addressed those watching by television. He said, "You can do what hundreds here are doing tonight. In the privacy of your own home or wherever you are, you can surrender your life to Christ. He said, "If you make that decision tonight, write to me, Billy Graham, Minneapolis, Minnesota; that's all the address you'll need."

I turned off the set, lit a candle, and sat on the floor and prayed a simple prayer. I asked Jesus to come into my life and forgive me of my sin. I told Him the door was open, and I wanted Him to come into my heart and take over my life. I had made a mess of my life, and I was willing to surrender to Him.

I felt something deep inside me that I had never felt before. I couldn't explain it, but it felt great. I had a deep-seated peace that this was it, and I had found the answer to my questions. I had a sense of hope that I couldn't explain either. I just knew that my life was going to be different.

The next day, I found myself reading more and more of the Bible, and it was making sense. A friend of mine drove up that afternoon on his motorcycle. I explained to him what had happened. He seemed surprised that I would be talking to God but said, "Hey, that's cool!"

That night, he said, "Let's hit the bars." I didn't want to. He couldn't believe it. "What's wrong with you?"

"I think I'm going to just stay here and watch Billy Graham again tonight." He kept shaking his head in disbelief and finally went by himself.

I watched again. When he got back, I was all excited to tell him what Billy had talked about that night. He seemed more startled and puzzled by my interest than disinterested himself. He seemed glad that I had found something that I thought would help me.

I went back, after those three days, with an assurance that something significant had happened in my life. I tried to explain it to my parents, my family, and my girlfriend. They all seemed happy for me but didn't really have a clue what I was talking about.

In my mind, I was the only one who knew what this was about . . . me and all those people who went to the front on the telecast. I couldn't think of anyone I knew that would understand. I wrote to that Minneapolis address, and they sent me some follow-up information and a basic Bible study from the Book of John.

Every day, I would spend some time with the Bible study and look up verses to find the answers to fill in the blanks or answer the questions. I sent them in and they sent them back. It helped me get started in my understanding of what had happened to me, where to go from here, and how to grow.

It's not like everything just got better. There were a lot of struggles, old feelings, and lonely nights crying in my room. But there was hope that I hadn't had before. I also could see and sense some changes in my life and in my heart that assured me-- He was there and was at work.

Chapter 7

COAST GUARD DAYS

In February 1976, I boarded a plane heading for USCG boot camp in Cape May, New Jersey. I had never been on a plane before or out of the State of Wisconsin. This was all new and scary for me. I was a mama's boy and didn't want to leave. It was so hard that day at Austin Straubel Airport in Green Bay to say goodbye to my family and to my girlfriend.

Boot camp was abrupt. I had retained my shoulder length hair from my drug days. One of the first items of business was to put me in a barber chair, facing a huge mirror, and watch as they, row by row, buzzed off all my hair. I looked totally different. I didn't even recognize myself. I cried as I watched it fall from my head to the ground. My golden-blondish-brown hair had been awfully important to me. That was just the beginning of sorrows. The commanding officers were mean and insensitive . . . and sometimes downright cruel. Their intent was to strip you of any independence and any sense of dignity you thought you had. I felt like dirt. The training was hard in the classroom and physically, but nothing compared to the emotional and psychological turmoil they put you through. Ten weeks of this!! I cried myself to sleep almost every night wishing I could just go home. The gravity of the four-year commitment I had made was definitely sinking in.

A few weeks into boot camp, I got a shocking letter from my girlfriend. We had plans of marriage and vowed we would be there for each other. She had been sending letters to me daily, and I was sending mine daily to her to be picked up at my parents' home. Her parents told her before I left we couldn't write, so we worked around it. Her parents found some letters I had sent addressed to her at my parents' house and were furious with her. They made her write a letter in their presence telling me it was off and that she would not be writing anymore. Perhaps in a few years, after she got out of high school and I out of the military, then we could see each other.

I didn't realize how addicted I was to her until we had been separated and now cut off. I felt like my heart was being torn in half. The horrors of boot camp, along with being away from home, and now the news from her seemed to be too much; but it drove me to God. I found myself crying out to Him and turning to Him constantly. I would go for long walks and talk to Him like He was my best friend. I sensed His presence, His love, and His friendship in new ways. I also found myself reading the Bible like I couldn't get enough. I started attending chapel on base and met a few other guys who seemed a bit interested in God.

Out of boot camp, I took a billet on a ship in Portland, Maine. It was the Coast Guard Cutter Duane, a 327, wartime ship. When I went aboard, an officer offered to show me around the ship. As he showed me around, he noted two guys sitting together on a bunk and said, "Stay away from those guys."

"Why?" I inquired.

"Because they are Jesus freaks." I asked what a Jesus freak was. "They are people who are really into God." *Cool*, I thought to myself, and made a point to introduce myself to them later.

When I did, they were very warm and receptive. They invited me to go to a Bible study with them.

"What is a Bible study?" I asked.

"It's where you go to a place with other Christians to study the Bible together."

"Oh." That sounded great to me, so I went with them, and it was great.

This Bible study was a part of a church I started attending, whenever I could, when we were in port. I met a couple who lived on a farm that really took me in. They had a few kids of their own, a little younger than I, but they welcomed me into their family. They said anytime I wanted to come and stay with them, I was welcomed to, and even gave me a key and said, if they weren't home to help myself. They became my first spiritual parents, who just loved me and wanted to help me grow.

We had great talks about the Bible and certain verses in particular. Their last name is Moulten, and I ended up calling them Ma and Pa Moulten. For the year and a half I spent in Maine, they were my family and demonstrated, in very practical and personal ways to me, the love and acceptance of Christ. They were my first experience of seeing the gospel fleshed out and of tasting what Christian community was like. They loved the people of the church they were a part of and were very committed to witnessing and sharing Christ with anyone who didn't know Him yet. Pa Moulten had a real pastor's heart, and from him, I had my first experience of being shepherded by a godly leader. I am eternally grateful to the whole Moulten family for taking me in, loving and accepting me, and for their investment in my life in those early days, when I was just learning to go from a crawl to a walk. They helped teach me how to walk.

There were a few other fellow shipmates that were believers that really helped me, too. We had great times of fellowship and encouragement and times in the Word together.

When I first went aboard that ship, I found out we were going on a three-month excursion called a cadet cruise. This is where we would pick up a load of officers in school at the Academy in New London, Connecticut, and give them three months of on-hands training and experience. We sailed across the ocean and pulled into ports on

Malaga, Spain; Rota, Spain; Portsmouth, England; and Naples, Italy. Sailing through the Straits of Gibraltar was fun and imagining where the Bermuda Triangle was, intriguing.

Those ports were interesting in being exposed to different countries and cultures; but " port" meant mostly one thing to most crew members – major, massive party time. Off they'd go and come back drunk, stoned, or tripping on something, along with wild stories of all the women they got that night.

The hardest part of those first three months was that the few other believers I had met, when I first got aboard, had been placed at the land station in South Portland for the duration of the cruise. To my knowledge, I was one of the only believers on the ship and a brand-new, naive one at that. It became known that I was a Christian. I was very quiet, shy, and insecure at this time and not very vocal, but some took it upon themselves to oppose me. They would do all sorts of things to get at me and mock me for my faith.

They did the normal pranks they do with many of the new guys; like the time I was new on duty in the fire room. They told me to go to the engine room to get some prop wash. I inquired in the engine room, and they told me I had to go to the bridge for it. I went to the bridge, and they sent me to the deck crew. Eventually, I caught on. It's funny as I think about it now – prop wash?

One time, I opened my locker, and there were a bunch of centerfolds and pin-ups from a Playboy in there with my name written on them. Several guys were positioned for, when I opened it, to call attention to it and ask me where I got them. Before I knew it, there were a handful of guys standing around, asking me questions and laughing. There were often comments made about me being a Jesus freak, especially when I didn't partake in their parties or porn flicks in the mess deck late at night.

It was a hard time but a good time. Though I felt very lonely and scared, I spent lots of time alone with God. I would spend countless hours on the fantail of the ship late at night gazing at the stars and connecting with God. I also got permission from a chief to use his office when he wasn't in there. I spent tons of time in there studying scripture. I would do word studies and cross reference and just dig into the Word. I learned so much and grew like crazy. I also was hiding the Word in my heart and memorizing scripture. It was so renewing.

That year and a half on the ship was a real time of preparation. I often refer to that time as my Bible school days. Because I had few friends and not much to do, I'd spend many hours every day studying scripture, praying, and getting to know God. It was a time of really establishing my personal, vertical relationship with God Himself. I really got to know Him well during this time.

I got transferred to a buoy tender-icebreaker in Sturgeon Bay, Wisconsin, on Lake Michigan. The ship was 180 feet long with a crew of about 40-50 guys. We set the buoys for the majority of the west side of Lake Michigan in that area and up through the Bay of Green Bay. There were a few believers on board that became friends. When we were in port on weekends, I would try to get home, which was about two hours away.

My contact with my family had been minimal up until now. They thought I'd flipped out and gone extreme in this religious thing. I must admit, I came on like gangbusters with them and did a lot to push them away from what I wanted so badly to bring them to. I was quite judgmental and legalistic with them. By this time, I was starting to mellow, which allowed them to see some of the genuine changes that had occurred in my life. My father had once commented that everything I did, I did extreme, and now I'm into this God thing in extreme. That hurt, but I knew he didn't understand.

When I first got to Maine and attended a church that was different from the one I grew up in, they were quite worried and concerned. They tried to set it up to get a pastor from the church I grew up in to come to visit me and persuade me to go back to that church. Often, when I was home on leave, I would get into arguments with my mom about what church I was a part of. She'd often ask me in tears, "How can you do this to your father and me?"

I would say, "I'm not doing this to hurt you or as a statement against your church. I just need to be a part of a church that I believe is teaching the Bible and helping me grow as a Christian."

When I started coming home on weekends from Sturgeon Bay, I started attending charismatic prayer meetings with my mom. Through a series of events and those meetings, I believe my mother came to faith in Christ and came to know Jesus in a personal way. It was just a matter of time until my brother, Bob, then brother Jim, then my father would all came to a place of personal faith themselves. Even my sister, Lois, in her way, came to Christ and to listen to her today, there is no doubt she has a personal relationship herself with Christ. Each in my family has their own story to tell of how God worked in their lives to bring them to Himself.

After serving on the buoy tender on Sturgeon Bay for over a year, I got transferred to a small duty station in Menasha, Wisconsin, to finish out my term. The station was just 15 minutes from where I grew up, and I never knew it was there. There were only five men at the station; it was a small Aids to Navigation Station. We basically set and maintained buoys in major waterways on the Fox and Wolf Rivers in the spring and summer and picked them up in the fall. I lived at home while spending my last year or so in the U.S. Military.

One of my first weeks there, I was driving home and drove past a church building; the sign said it was a nondenominational church. I checked it out the next Sunday, and it seemed consistent with what I had known so far. I started attending regularly and getting involved. I discovered the church had also started a Christian radio station, and I volunteered my time to help. I'd run errands and just pitch in to help in any way that I could. The senior pastor was also the station manager, and he always found things for me to help out with. They also owned a bookstore, and I remember going there to help with chores and cleanup. Before long, I was asked to share my testimony at a Sunday evening service. I was delighted to and was amazed that some people responded and wanted to receive Christ at the end of that service.

I was also involved in the prayer meetings of the congregation that my parents belonged to. I was asked by the pastor and a deacon in that church if I would consider starting a youth group for the youth of that parish. I was delighted to. We met weekly on Tuesday evenings and had a time of song and worship, prayer, and a teaching. Many youth were coming and discovering Christ personally.

One of my favorite stories is about a family that had moved to our village mid-school year. The mother had tried to get her kids enrolled in the church's religious education classes but was unable to. She had heard about this youth group and made her 16-year-old son attend as an alternative to him not getting into the regular classes. He was a druggie, and the first night he came, he came in stoned and not knowing what to expect. He sat through the music and thought it strange. Then, the message that night was about eternity and where you will spend it. He had heard things he'd never really considered before, and it got him thinking, though it scared him. He kept coming back because his mom made him go, and within five or six weeks, he had opened his heart and invited Jesus to come into his life.

Chapter 8

BIBLE SCHOOL

One of my friends invited me to go to a David
Wilkerson Crusade. Dallas Holm did a music
set, and David preached and gave an invitation;
hundreds went forward that night to receive Christ.
Somewhere during the course of the evening,
David mentioned a Bible training school they had
in Lindale, Texas. If anyone was interested, there
were brochures in the back. I picked one up and
read it, and it seemed to be just what I was looking
for. I had been planning, ever since I'd been in the
Coast Guard, to go to a Bible school when I got
discharged.

I applied for the school in November 1979. I was to be discharged from the Coast Guard in early February 1980, and the school was to begin mid-February 1980. The timing seemed ideal. Within a few weeks after I applied, I got a call saying the school only took 50 applicants, and it had been filled up for months, but they would put my name on a long waiting list. I was disappointed but thought God must have something different for me. About one month later, I received a call from the director of the school, Dr. Charles Snow, telling me someone had dropped out and of all the applicants on the waiting list, they sensed through prayer, they were to offer the opening to me. My father offered to put up some money for the costs, and all the lights seemed to be green. I was discharged from the Coast Guard and left a week later for the Institute of Christian Training School, 90 miles east of Dallas.

The school was just a little over four months long but was packed with excellent and practical teaching. Some of the courses included classes like

Effective Communication, How to Minister to Drug Addicts and Alcoholics, Effective Teaching, Principles of Biblical Leadership, Principles of Effective Evangelism. I was eating it up. I studied and applied myself and got good grades. The teachers were exceptional, especially Dr. Charles Snow and Dr. Ken Mayton, our two in-house teachers. They also brought in other great teachers.

I met some great students from all over the country with hearts bent on reaching the drug subculture with the gospel. We also went on several outreach trips, one to San Antonio, Texas, and one to inner city Denver, Colorado. We worked with the Teen Challenge Centers in those areas. Teen Challenge has an 86% cure rate for drug addicts that go through and finish their program. The government put out a movie documenting the success of Teen Challenge called The Jesus Factor. It showed that the success of Teen Challenge was because of Jesus, and it was a personal encounter with the risen Christ that gave addicts the power to truly change.

It was a life-changing, life-challenging and equipping time for me. I could hardly wait to get back and get to work. When I returned, I had ideas of starting a Christian coffeehouse and outreach center.

STREET MINISTRY

I reconnected with some friends from the church, and I rejoined them in their weekly gatherings. Within a few weeks, a handful of us went to a big Christian concert. At break time, we stood around the record table discussing how blessed we were at the concert. Then someone said, "Yeah, but what about all the people 'out there' who have no idea who Jesus is?"

That small handful of us left the concert at the break and headed to downtown Appleton to assess the need out on the streets. We were amazed at how many teens were hanging out on the streets and how many young adults were hopping from bar to bar. The need was slapping us in the face, and we vowed we were going to do something regularly. We started meeting on Friday nights in the parking lot next to the big chapel on the campus of Lawrence University. We would get in a circle, pray, then have a brief planning discussion and hit the streets. We had some relevant gospel tracts, but our main goal was to strike up conversations with people that would lead to a discussion about the gospel. We were amazed with the general receptivity of people to what we had to say.

Our little team going out on Friday and Saturday nights grew as others joined us to hit the streets. Some would stay back and pray. We started to pray with people to receive Christ on the streets and in downtown bars. We started looking for a downtown building to use as a base for our efforts. A few of us met to pray. We decided we needed a name, so we voted on names and came up with Solid Rock Ministries, our slogan – *Going to where the people are with what the people need.*

About the same time all of this was starting, the senior pastor of the church I was attending, Arthur Gregg, called and asked if he could meet me for lunch. We met, and he asked me if I would consider being the youth pastor at the church. He said, "The youth group is small, but it needs someone to lead it. If you will commit to being there for the youth on Sundays and Wednesdays, then whatever else you want to do in developing the street ministry would be okay with me." I thought it was an ideal offer.

The offices for the church staff were combined with the offices of the Christian radio station. When I started working there I met, among others, the pastor's oldest daughter who worked for the station. I had seen her before while she was interpreting for the deaf at church services but hadn't met her. I found her to be gentle and sweet and easy to talk to. We got along well, and I would occasionally ask her to do things for me because I didn't have any secretarial help. She seemed happy to do so.

Every Monday morning, the general manager of the station had me on a half hour spot called *The People's Program*. We would talk about youth and their needs, what was happening on the streets, and the Bible studies in the public high schools. One morning, we talked about the need for a base to go from for the teams going out into the streets on Friday and Saturday evenings. We got a call immediately from the captain of the Salvation Army offering us the use of their building, which was close to downtown.

I was on staff only a month or two when a problem arose, and the senior pastor resigned. It was a time of a lot of hurt and confusion for everyone. I didn't know the pastor very well or the board members. It was also a very difficult time for the pastor's daughter, and I tried to be there for her to listen and encourage. We started spending quite a bit of time together, and she would often ask me if we were dating. I'd quickly respond with a resounding "NO," and clarified that we were just friends, and I was committed to being like Paul, free to devote myself to full-time ministry. I backed it up with I Corinthians 7, which says that it is better to remain single. I simply was not being honest with myself or with her. I'll never forget the time she asked me if it is common for friends, a brother and sister in Christ, to kiss each other. My reaction was to resolve to not kiss her anymore, but her question was all I needed to help me be more realistic.

Our relationship developed, and we were married on February 27, 1981. I had proposed to her while on a winter retreat with just 15 of us in Eagle River, Wisconsin. We had determined before we left for our honeymoon that I was to resign from the youth pastor position with the church and go full-time with the developing street and outreach ministry called Solid Rock.

The transition was on good terms, and the church leadership concurred that was where I best fit. The captain from the Salvation Army had offered a little 12'x15' office to us at no charge to get started,

Solid Rock Ministries – Reaching and Restoring the Hurting to Wholeness in Christ.

We are eternally grateful to Captain Fred Eames and his wife, Beth, who was also a Salvation Army officer, for their generosity, kindness, and encouragement. Offering us the use of the building and giving us free office space was a huge factor in helping us get the ministry off the ground. Their support and encouragement helped us believe that God did want to use us in reaching out to this generation with hope and help in Jesus' Name.

SOLID ROCK OFFICIALLY BEGINS

The second week of March 1981 found me with a volunteer secretary, sitting in our new office space with a few donated desks, a filing cabinet, and two telephones. The black phone was our regular line, and the red phone was our crisis line; we called it Life Line. We manned it at the office during the day and call-forwarded to homes of trained individuals in the evening. I remember the first couple of weeks just kind of twiddling our thumbs, looking at each other, waiting for the phone to ring. It didn't take long before it was ringing all the time. I spent the majority of my time answering phones, meeting with people for counseling and discipleship, and following up on people we had met on the streets over the weekend. The teams going out on Friday evenings grew at one point to 35-40 people. Some would stay back and pray and oversee the drop-in center, but most would go out two-by-two on the streets and into bars looking for opportunity to strike up a conversation and tell people about Jesus.

After about a year and a half, we did some evaluation. We had the names and addresses of many people that we had led to Christ. After we prayed with them to receive Christ, we would try to get them into a Bible study and refer them to a good church in town. We had about 150 names in our files, so we started to call them to see how they were doing in their walk with God. We discovered that only a small handful had actually connected to a local church. Some had connected with as a para-church ministry and got involved, but most weren't connected anywhere and were not growing. That troubled us.

After much prayer and discussion, we contacted a few Christian leaders we knew to get some input. One of them was Don Wilkerson. I had met Don when I was in Texas at the Bible School. We had corresponded a few times, and he had given some great advice regarding our outreach ministry. He had been involved with street work nearly 25 years by then and had been an Executive Director of the original Teen Challenge in Brooklyn for about as many years. He helped shepherd us during this time of transition and development. He flew in a few times to meet with leaders, to pray with us, and to dialog with us about what we sensed God was saying.

A verse came alive to us at this time: I Corinthians 4:15; Paul said to the Corinthians,

> *You have 10,000 instructors in Christ but no fathers. I begot you in the gospel, be ye followers of me. (KJV).*

Through this verse, a series of events, some godly input from respected leaders, especially Don Wilkerson, and what we believed was the nudging of the Holy Spirit, we felt we were supposed to start a church.

We had tons of questions and even more doubts. None of us had been to seminary, and none of us had any formal training in church planting; we felt we didn't have a clue on how to do this. What we did know was we loved God, we were seeing people come to Christ regularly, and we knew they needed to be raised in the gospel and nurtured in the faith. We also felt that God was telling us that if we were going to "give birth" to people in the gospel, we also needed to assume parental responsibility in raising them once they were born. So, we just launched out in faith with what we did know and trusted that God would lead, guide, and provide as we went along.

We stood strong on a few verses. One was Psalm 127:1, which says,

> *Unless the Lord build the house, they labor in vain that build it. Unless the Lord keep the city, they guard it in vain.*

The other verse was Ecclesiastes 3:14,

> *Whatever God does, it shall be forever. Nothing shall be added to it and nothing shall be taken away from it. God does it that men would fear before Him.*

With deep feelings of inadequacy and uncertainty, we moved forward primarily in obedience to what we sensed God was telling us to do.

OUTSTANDING ALUMNI AWARD

It was at about this same time that I received a phone call from my former assistant football coach and guidance counselor. He told me that all of the teachers from junior and senior high have a banquet once a year, and among other things, they give out an award to the most outstanding alumni. He said at a recent meeting he had nominated me, and it was unanimous to give me the award that year. He told me when the date was and asked me to prepare a 10-minute speech describing how my life had changed so dramatically. I was delighted to.

That evening he awarded me with the plaque and introduced me to the crowd as Pastor Bill Lenz. I thanked everyone and said, "Before anything else, I need to apologize."

As I looked out, I saw the faces of many teachers I had in high school. "I need to first say a few words to those of you who had me as a student. I am sorry for being such a rebellious and disrespectful student. I made your jobs much harder than they should have been. You put up with a lot from me."

Several of them by name, I asked to forgive me. I also thanked Coach and Guidance Counselor Bud Kohn for being there for me when I was at my worst and for planting seeds about the gospel in me and praying for me. Then, I simply shared how I had become a Christian and how it was Christ who changed my life not me. Again, what a joy and privilege it was to tell of what He had done for me.

Chapter 9

THE HUGO STRUCK STORY

One weekend while I was still in the Coast Guard, I was at the cottage with my parents. I went for a drive past an old farm house that jogged my memory. I had flashbacks of having been in that house before. Bit by bit, I remembered when.

During the summer between my junior and senior year in high school, a druggie buddy and myself spent a few days at the cottage. We were running low on drugs, and my buddy came up with an idea...he suggested we go knock on some farm house doors. If someone came to the door, we'd ask if they knew where Fred Jones lived or some other fictitious name. When they said, "no, never heard of him," we'd say, "okay, thanks" and leave. If we knocked on the door and no one was home, we'd enter the house, help ourselves to some goods, and then go into town and deal for drugs.

So here I am, driving past this farm house remembering four or five years earlier what we stole from there....a chainsaw, three or four shotguns, and some milk cans. I sensed the Spirit of God speaking to me, telling me I needed to go back to that house and apologize and make restitution. I wrestled with it for a few weeks and finally found the courage to go back.

It was after work on a Tuesday night that a Christian friend and I drove out to the farm. She agreed to stay in my little brown Honda Civic and pray while I went to the door. I was scared. Finally, I knocked on the door and the inside door slowly creaked as it slowly opened. I couldn't believe what I saw... an old man, standing about 6'8", weighing well over 300 pounds standing in the doorway. He had gray hair, a crew cut, and was wearing bib overalls. I thought to myself, *I need to get out of here while I'm alive.* I wanted so badly to just run. Couldn't I just ask God to forgive me and send some money to charity and call it even?

A deep, gravelly voice uttered, "Can I help you?"

I stuttered and stammered, "Yes, um, um, um…. can I come in?"

"Come in? What for, I don't even know you!"

"I know, I'm sorry. Well, sir, I'm here to say I'm sorry. You see, I was here about four or five years ago with a friend, and we took some things out of your house, and I'm here to say I'm sorry and pay you back."

He instantly grabbed me, pulled me to the back hallway and threw me to floor. He was swearing and cursing and threatening to teach me a lesson.

His wife came running out yelling, "Hugo, Hugo, what's going on back here?"

He said, "This no good, blankety blank was the one that robbed our home!"

She immediately asked, "Well, why did he come back?" He shrugged.

I piped up quickly…"I'm here to apologize and to pay you back for all the things we stole from you." Hugo was still fuming, but she was inquisitive.

She asked, "What would make you want to come back and do this?"

"Well, ma'am, a few years ago I became a Christian, and Jesus radically changed my life. I've become a brand-new person. I was reminded of what I had done before, and I believe Jesus told me to come back here to apologize and to pay you back." She shuttered in disbelief.

Hugo was still waiting to teach me a lesson. She told Hugo to let me up from the floor so we could sit at the table to talk about this. Hugo reluctantly agreed.

Hugo went to the refrigerator and grabbed an article from the newspaper that reported the break-in five years earlier. "We have lived in fear ever since this happened. My wife has been afraid to stay here alone in her own home. I've had to take her with me everywhere I went or have one of our grown children or neighbors come and stay with her."

I saw the fear and pain in their eyes. My own eyes filled with tears as I said I was so very sorry. "There is no excuse for what I did. I'm sorry I put you through this. I'm asking you to forgive me."

At that she said, "Oh, it's okay sonny. Now tell us again what happened in your life and how you changed."

I told them the whole story of being at the cottage and reading about being born again in John 3 and listening to Billy Graham on TV. I told them how I prayed a prayer and invited Jesus into my life and how my life has not been the same since.

We had a great talk and worked out arrangements for me to make payments each month until I paid them back. Once a month, I'd drive out to make my payment. When I'd drive in the driveway, they'd come out to greet me and offer me something to drink and to come in for awhile. They said they looked forward to my visits. Several times since, I wondered about calling my old buddy and having him cough up the cash for his half......but I never did.

Several months later, I got a call from the pastor of the church not far from Hugo's farm. It was an old, rural country church. The pastor heard about me going to Hugo and what I shared with them. He asked if I would come and share my story with their congregation at a Sunday service.

I'll never forget that day. I brought some other young adults and youth along to do some contemporary worship. That morning the little country church was packed. Some of the people I knew from growing up in the summer at the cottage and rabbit hunting in that area were there. Just near the back sat Hugo and his wife and grown children. The pastor couldn't believe they came because the church they went to forbid members from ever stepping foot in another church. But there they were with wide grins.

What a privilege it was for me to stand in front of that congregation and tell about how I met the Savior and how He had changed my life......just down the street from where just five years earlier I was stealing to buy drugs. I told everyone there that morning that Jesus could change their lives, too, and give them eternal life if they would humble themselves and invite Him in.

Chapter 10

THE BIRTH OF A CHURCH

We searched for a place to meet. We found a little cobblestone chapel at Riverside Cemetery along the Fox River in Appleton, Wisconsin. It had old mahogany pews and seated up to 90. The owners were willing to rent it to us for five dollars a week, and two dollars a week for electricity. The first Sunday we gathered, there were 13 people. Jeff Jansen from the youth group was our worship leader. He knew three chords on the guitar. My wife, Janet, sat in the front pew with a keyboard on her lap to contribute to the worship. She didn't like being up in front so we designated the front pew for her.

We started Sunday School classes for the children during the services. They met down in the cellar next to the furnace with some benches. On nice days, they would meet out among the tombstones and sit on the grass.

Janet recalls the time she was in the cellar teaching a lesson on creation to the children. She noticed something swooping so she told the children to duck because there were some birdies flying around. Well, they were bats. A father of one of the kids came down and took care of the bats. When asked his name, he said, "You can call me Batman!"

The name of our church was The New Corinthian Chapel. We got our name from I Corinthians 6:9-11. It says,

> *Or do you not know that the unrighteous shall not inherit the Kingdom of God. Do not be deceived, neither fornicators, nor idolaters, nor adulterers, nor effeminate, nor homosexuals, nor thieves, nor covetous, nor drunkards, nor*

> *revilers, nor swindlers shall inherit the Kingdom*
> *of God. And such were some of you, but you*
> *were washed, but you were sanctified, but you*
> *were justified in the name of the Lord Jesus*
> *Christ and in the Spirit of our God.*

Because of our ministry in the bars and on the streets, most of the people who were coming into the church had these kinds of backgrounds. The key part of the verse is, "And such were some of you, but you were washed and sanctified and justified." We had met Jesus, and He forgave our sin and changed our lives. We were new creatures in Christ.

We were like those who had been converted in Corinth. So, we were the New Corinthians, who had been given a new nature, and had been made new creations. II Corinthians 5:17 (KJV) says,

> *Therefore, if any man is in Christ, he is a new*
> *creature, the old things passed away; behold all*
> *things have become new.*

We now had a place to invite people to once they had given their lives to Christ. Often, we'd talk to someone about Jesus or lead them to Christ on a Friday or Saturday night, then pick them up for services on Sunday morning. We had small groups and Bible studies going during the week to help people study the Scriptures and get needed fellowship. In about a year, we had outgrown Riverside Cemetery Chapel.

We looked for a new place to meet. Right on the main drag in downtown Appleton was an old theatre called The Viking Theatre. We inquired and came to an agreement for $175 a month. This was a huge jump for us, but it included heating and water. We had to set up equipment each week for services, as well as for classes for children. We held classes in hallways, stairwells, and entrances to restrooms. It was easy to invite people we talked with on the streets Friday and Saturday nights to check out one of our services on Sunday. Many of them did, and the church continued to grow. What was exciting to us was that the church was growing because those who had been far from God were being introduced to Jesus and then becoming a part of the church. Way too often churches grow through transfer growth – where people are already Christians who leave their church to become part of this "growing" church. What was happening reminded me of Acts 2:47,

> *And the Lord was adding to their number day*
> *by day, those who were being saved.*

Each one had a remarkable story of how they were lost and without hope . . . and how they had met the Risen Savior and He forgave their sin, and He was radically changing their lives. They would also tell of how they had been accepted into a family and treated with kindness and grace. They would speak of the delight of experiencing being a part of the wonder of Christian community and being loved like they never had been before. Were we experiencing a modern-day version of what happened in Acts chapter two, as the Church was being the Church?

STORIES OF LIFE CHANGE

Our crisis line, Lifeline, had been going for several years. A well-known realtor from our area had heard about our work and was especially moved by stories he had heard about those who had gotten help by calling Lifeline. He wanted to get involved. He offered to underwrite the cost of having Lifeline messages put up on billboards on major streets and highways throughout our area. One had a picture of a big red heart with a crack running through it. On the side of it, in huge letters, was the word HURTING? Then it said, "Call Lifeline 734-2323. For anyone who needs to talk to someone, anytime." Another billboard had a picture of a life ring with a rope. The caption on the side read, "Reach for the Lifeline – call 734-2323." We would get all sorts of calls from those who were suicidal, determined that taking their life was the only option, to people calling for directions or asking how to get their lawnmower started. Most calls were from those who were hurting and needed someone to talk to.

SARAH'S STORY

One day, I opened the mail and there was a handwritten letter from Sarah recalling what had taken place just a few months earlier. She was 20, and her life was falling apart. Her mother had died six months earlier, and Sarah had dropped out of college. Her boyfriend and fiancée of three years broke up with her, and she was in major pain. She had gone to a party on a Friday night to try to forget her sorrows. As she drank a few beers and tried talking to a few friends, she felt so alone and isolated. She was feeling worse and worse, and her despair was overtaking her. She left the party and was determined to take her life. She walked to the Oneida Street Bridge near downtown Appleton. She stood in the middle of the bridge, trying to work up the courage to jump. Tears were streaming down her face as she was counting down. Through the tears, she looked up and saw a billboard with a big heart and a crack in the heart. She read the word – Hurting? – and saw the phone number. She argued back and forth with herself

107

for several minutes then decided . . . why not call? What do I have to lose?

She walked away from the bridge and found a pay phone. She called the number and spoke to a woman who at one time had been suicidal herself. She listened, understood, cared, and cried with Sarah. Sarah was feeling better already with a sense of hope. Then, the woman began to share with Sarah how she had come to know Jesus personally, and how He had given her Hope and changed her life. Sarah prayed over the phone with this woman to receive Christ.

The next day, the woman picked Sarah up and took her to lunch. They met every week for a Bible study to help Sarah grow in her new-found faith in Christ. Sarah was writing to me to thank us for starting Solid Rock and for having Lifeline there for her when she needed it. She wrote of her story and the radical difference Jesus was making in her life. What a joy it was, months later, to witness Sarah being water-baptized and personally identify with the death, burial, and resurrection of Jesus Christ. How exciting it was to see Sarah in a worship service, worshipping her Savior with other freshly redeemed people. It wasn't long before Sarah was helping out in our children's ministry . . . demonstrating the love of Christ to 4- and 5-year-olds.

Let me tell you, it is stories like this that make it all worth it. The bottom line of why we do what we do in ministry is to see lost people genuinely converted and begin a lifelong relationship with a loving Savior. To watch lives change before your eyes is evidence of the power of the gospel. That is what it is all about.

The church continued to grow at the Viking Theatre. We had to expand classes for the children. We rented rooms across the street above a Chinese restaurant. They were abandoned apartments that, with a little fixing up, worked well for classrooms. I remember seeing teachers bundling up children in winter jackets and then marching them across the street and up a flight of stairs to their classrooms. No one complained. There was a sense of excitement and privilege that we were able to be a part of teaching the Bible to young children. No one cared that the conditions were not very good. What mattered most was happening, and we were thrilled to be a part of it.

One thrill for the children, while we were meeting at the theatre, was that as the services were ending, the theatre staff was preparing for their Sunday afternoon matinees! The smell of fresh popcorn filled the air, and attendants would offer free popcorn to cute and innocent children on their way out from the service.

There would be Sundays that we would come into the theatre to get ready for services and posters advertising the movies would be quite offensive. So, we would get permission to take them down until after our services. Often, people in walking to their seats would feel their shoes stick to the floor from spilled pop from the night before.

Conditions weren't great, but that didn't limit or hinder the moving of the Holy Spirit in our services. What a thrill it was to watch God round up a bunch of messed up, broken people, and fill them with His Spirit, and start teaching us what it meant to worship Him and love each other.

We met in the Viking Theatre for nearly two years. Then a building that was close to downtown opened up. It had originally been built and occupied by a Lutheran church in town. When they moved, a local repertory theater group moved in, painted everything black, and built a huge stage. The theater group couldn't keep it going and closed it down and boarded it shut. An upstart church with a few handfuls of people moved in and started remodeling and repainting. They assumed a mortgage with the original church that owned it. When they couldn't make it go, it was offered to us to assume the $89,000 mortgage in a land contract. It seemed so out of reach, but we sensed God had given us the nod to move on it. We now had a place to call home and a bit of a sense of permanency.

We kept all of our outreach ministries going and still had teams going on the streets weekends and had our Lifeline. At its peak, our Lifeline averaged 10 calls per day, often from hurting seekers very open to the gospel. What we learned quickly was by having services, we opened wide another means of reaching people who were far from God.

People who were a part of the church were so excited about what God was doing in their own lives and what God was doing in the church; they would automatically invite family members, friends, neighbors and coworkers to come to church services with them. As they'd come, they'd sense God's presence among His people, hear His Word, and would be drawn to Christ. It became a regular occurrence to see people accept Christ at the end of our services. He continued to add daily to the church those being saved.

Our goal was to reach people for Christ and then see them followed up on, discipled, and helped to grow in their relationship with God by getting connected and becoming an active, contributing part of a loving Christian community.

We were convinced that God had designed the Church, and every believer needed to be plugged into a local church and flesh out the gospel we believed, in how we lived, and how we loved each other. From the beginning, we emphasized love and unity in Christian community. Jesus clearly stated, in John 13:34-35,

> *A new commandment I give unto you, that you love each other the way I have loved you. By this all men will know you are My disciples, because you love one another.*

Jesus also told us that the world would know that He was sent by the Father, by the unity of oneness of His followers (John 17:21). That was a huge value to us, and we upheld that value as a priority.

113

When there was conflict, we addressed it head on, so as to work it through to a place of resolution and restoration. We were big in not pretending and acting like all was fine if it wasn't. We were committed to honesty . . . a relational integrity. Our desire was to love each other just as Jesus was loving us. Then as others would come into the Church, we would invite them to partake of the joys of community but also teach them to be participants who contributed to community as well.

Through the years, we have maintained a relational emphasis that prioritizes loving well and demonstrates the acceptance of Christ in very personal and practical ways. Our emphasis is best summed up in our church slogan, "Loving God, loving others." This captures the essence of what Jesus taught were the two greatest commandments.

A LUMBERYARD

We continued to grow and see people come to Christ and become a part of the Church Family. We had three Sunday services and had added a Saturday evening service. We had maxed out our facilities and were considering our options. Years earlier, we had purchased 23 acres of land on the south side of Appleton. When we looked into it, we discovered it would be four or five more years before sewer and water would be there. One of our elders had seen a building that was boarded up and for sale that had housed a Wicks Lumber Company retail store. We looked at it, and the design of the building was quite unusual for a lumber store, but we envisioned it working well for a church to meet in. It would need a lot of remodeling, but it could work. We made an offer way below the asking price, contingent upon getting a loan, which they accepted. We couldn't believe it. But the bank we had been doing business with turned us down for a loan citing we were a newer church and didn't have a credit history. We were confused. We went to a different credit agency and got a loan but for $100,000 less than what we had offered originally. So, we rewrote our offer and submitted it; it was immediately accepted. Being turned down by a bank helped us save $100,000!

We began the remodeling project that lasted about nine months. The majority of all the work was done by volunteers within the Church body. Little did we know then how that would be used by God. It helped get a lot of people who weren't involved off the bench and into the game. It gave a sense of ownership to all who helped. It built unity and teamwork. New friendships had begun and were developing. We knew God was up to something big, and we were thrilled to be a part of it.

I will never forget that first Sunday in our newly remodeled building. There was electricity in the air and an excitement that was contagious. There was a sense that God wanted us to stretch out His arms a whole lot wider to our community and invite people to become a part of His family; and that is exactly what began to happen.

Chapter 11

A MISSING PERSON

Just a few months after moving into this newly remodeled building, a young 21-year-old girl had been reported missing. The Menasha Police Department had called us and asked if they could set up a makeshift headquarters for a search committee in trying to find Laurie Depies. We readily agreed and worked with the family and the police department to set up tables and telephones in our centrally located facility. Before we knew it, there were hundreds of volunteers coming in and out of our building, all trying to help find this missing person.

We were able to provide coffee, drinks, and snacks for the volunteers and were able to comfort and encourage family members distraught by the horror of what had happened. They all feared she had been abducted and taken hostage and were desperate for any signs of hope that she was still alive. Newspaper reporters and camera crews from TV stations were constantly reporting the story, and they always cited Christ The Rock Community Church as the headquarters for this search effort.

Our intent was to help a family and be available to help our community. Little did we know how God would use this event to put a good taste in peoples' mouths about this relatively unknown church in the community. Prior to this, our church was viewed with suspicion and question. Our area had a lot of denominational churches with a lot of tradition. Christ The Rock was a nondenominational church and was very nontraditional and outside of the box. Therefore, because it was different and there were a lot of unknowns about us, people in our community often were skeptical and considered us a cult. This event had done a lot to reverse the previous image.

Now, suddenly, we were known as the church that helped and headquartered the search for Laurie Depies. The search headquarters stayed in our building for about three months. Then, it simply went to the police department. Sadly, she never was found. After about one month into the search, her family asked us to do a prayer service for her. We did, and again, it was a great opportunity for us to serve the family in a time of crisis. Laurie's stepsister came to know Christ a few years later, and she testified that her experience with the church during her family's great time of loss had a huge part in helping her discover Jesus for herself. She is now a very active member of Christ The Rock and has a real heart to reach out to others who still don't know Jesus.

SOLID ROCK PHASES OUT

For the first seven or eight years we kept Solid Rock Ministries going as a separate nonprofit, para-church ministry. It was the vehicle that we used for outreach, our crisis line, speaking events in schools, civic clubs, and our counseling ministry.

My brother, Bob, had come on staff of Solid Rock after about two years. He also was the church's first youth pastor. He would do a lot of the speaking engagements. The more he spoke, the more he got invited. He realized his primary gifting was evangelism, and God was using him to reach a lot of youth through his speaking. He eventually resigned as youth pastor and went full-time with Solid Rock.

It was about this time that we sensed there was a season and a purpose for Solid Rock Ministries, but it was time for it to phase out. With Bob's speaking ministry really flourishing, we decided to give the nonprofit organization to Bob and to absorb some of the ministries of Solid Rock into the church. Bob changed the name to Life Promotions – It exists to convince youth that life is worth living to the fullest. Today, Bob is one of several speakers who have a speaking ministry through Life Promotions.

Bob, himself, speaks to about 150,000 youth per year primarily in public school settings. His message is one of hope, dealing with issues like suicide, drug and alcohol prevention, self-image, and other relevant topics. In the evenings, they do rallies that they invite the youth to come back out to and encourage them to bring their parents. In this setting, they are free to present the gospel and see hundreds of youth respond to Christ at most evening rallies. Life Promotions also sponsors a huge Christian music festival every July called Lifest in Oshkosh, Wisconsin. Bob is a dynamic and powerful speaker, and God uses him in great ways to reach youth for Christ.

EXPANDING OUR VISION

For about 12-13 years, our focus had been on reaching people for Christ within our immediate area . . . the Fox River Valley. My wife, Janet, started sharing about her desire for us to be more aware of what God was doing in other parts of the world as well. As we prayed, we sensed the Spirit's leading to take a trip and be exposed to the mission field. In May 1994, we headed out for five weeks to Western and Eastern Europe along with our three boys. At the time, they were 12, 10 and 7. We were in 11 different countries in that 5-week period. In most of the places we visited, we stayed with missionaries. We were in Croatia for six days.

At the time, there were 700,000 people living in refugee camps. We visited several and had the opportunity to speak and share the gospel with these refugees. One of the refugee camps we visited was in a former sports complex. It had a little diner on one end of the building. Our youngest son, Seth, got all excited thinking we would be able to order pizza. Boy, was he disappointed when he realized that was not a possibility. Then, they put us in front of the line as their honored guests to go through the meal line. The main dish that day was pea soup with big chunks of fat in the soup. It was considered a delicacy there. They even gave us extra. All three of our boys looked at us with a glance of despair and mouthed, "Do we have to eat this?"

Yes, we didn't want to offend these people who are giving their best for us. We sat across from an American missionary who had lived there for a few years. He joked with our boys about the food and why the chunks of fat had hair on them yet . . . because the pig had forgotten to shave that day. He graciously sneaked our boys' chunks into his bowl and ate the chunks for them. They were so grateful.

Romania was another eye-opener. We stayed with a native missionary. The average income for that part of Romania at the time was $50 a month. It opened our eyes to the incredible needs in that part of the world. The world had just gotten so much bigger so fast. We knew God was tugging on our hearts to be more aware and to get involved in reaching out to other countries as well.

Gradually, since that trip, our church has become more involved in world missions. Some countries we have been involved with include Romania, Western Sahara, Algeria, Sierra Leone, Mexico, Thailand, Haiti, India and others. Scripture is clear, we are to go into all the world and make disciples of all nations (Matthew 28:19-20).

STRENGTH WITHIN

In the eight years that we were in the lumber company building, we learned a lot. While our emphasis on outreach and evangelism continued, we were growing in learning how to be a "Church."

God always seemed to bring just the right people in to help add ingredients that were missing or weak. Larry Crabb and Dan Allender came in many times to help us grow in dealing with life honestly and learning how to grow in connecting and living out Christian community. Gayle Erwin repeatedly reminded us of the nature of Jesus and what it looks like to be more like Him. Stuart and Jill Briscoe kept reminding us of what local church was all about, how to build up leadership teams, how to stay soundly and profoundly biblical, and to hold by the value of preaching. They also helped remind us to stay globally conscious. Wes Roberts helped us with getting organized and clear about our purpose, vision, and values. Clive Calver helped us with being more aware of the poor and needy and how the Church is to be on the cutting edge of offering relief and development, as well as hope and help in Jesus' Name.

Reading Rick Warren's book helped us be more purpose-driven. Willow Creek conferences helped us think through being a prevailing Church, how to be more intentional in developing those who have the leadership gift, and how to be more creative in using the arts in communicating the gospel. John Dawson helped us with realizing the importance of reconciliation, especially in dealing with differences and past offenses between ethnic groups.

Henry Blackaby's book, *Experiencing God,* reminded us to look at what God is up to and joining in with Him, rather than coming up with our own plans and asking Him to bless them. We have learned so much from so many; and it has helped us develop as a church community. It would be foolish not to learn from each other.

THE NEXT MOVE

We knew for years that we were limited in our facility. Yet we were not eager or anxious to hurry up and get something bigger. Our goal had never been to be a big church but to keep winning people to Christ and helping them grow. Some churches have the philosophy, if you build it, they will come. Our philosophy was, if they keep coming, I guess we have to build it. We had looked into a dog track complex that had gone under. It had great potential and was on 100 acres of land. The owners were holding on to it with the hope that some Native Americans could get it and open a casino, so that door just didn't open to us.

Finally, we found an 80-acre piece of land only four miles away from our present location. It was priced at $12,000 an acre. It already had city sewer and water along the property. One family from the church put up the money to purchase the property with an interest-free loan!

Our executive pastor, Curt Drexler, drew up the original sketches for the design of the building that would best suit our needs. From there, we hired an architect and a building contractor. We looked for a contractor that would allow us to do as much volunteer labor as possible to help defray the costs. When all was said and done, we had over 900 people from our church help in some way with the new building. The volunteers saved the church about $350,000 in labor.

How exciting it was to see people willingly, joyfully, chipping in to help see this project completed. Again, we saw the miracle of teamwork at its best. There was a sense of ownership and accomplishment. There are several stories of men, who got involved in helping with building, who came to know Christ personally through the process. Many others developed new friendships, and others started small groups with those they had met while working together. Many guys, who were not previously involved, dove in and have been involved ever since. So many good things have come out of inviting volunteers to help with the building.

In May 2001, we held our first services in our new facility. Finally, we could breathe again, had room to grow, and could welcome in seekers and new visitors. The second week we were in the new building, we saw 150 people indicate first-time commitments to Christ at our weekend services.

About 4-1/2 months after we moved in, we all saw the tragedy of 9/11 and the terrorist attacks on the World Trade Center and the Pentagon. That following weekend, churches across America reported record attendance at their services. We were no exception. At our 10:30 a.m. service alone, we had over 1300 people. That is 500 more people than we could have seated in our old building just five months earlier.

It just confirmed so solidly to us that it was a necessary move. How could we put a price tag on the value of just one person coming to Christ? To what lengths will we go, and what expense will we sacrifice, to be a part of extending an invitation to lost people to consider the offer of the Gospel?

When I hear of individual stories of how God used our church to help someone come to Christ, it moves me to tears and I think, "This is what it's all about. This is why we exist as a church."

What a privilege it is to be invited by God to be a small part of what He is doing – seeking and saving that which is lost. Nothing brings joy to my heart quite like hearing newly redeemed people tell of how they fell into the scandal of Grace, and how Jesus has forever changed their lives and their destinies.

Often my wife, Janet, and I will look at each other and say, "Who would have thunk it?"

We stand absolutely amazed and humbled by what God has chosen to do. We feel so honored to be invited by Him, and included by Him, to be a part of His awesome work. Jesus is the One who said that HE would build His church and the gates of hell will not prevail against it (Matthew 16:18).

We know He wants His Church to prevail. We know He wants every local church to be healthy and balanced and to be on the cutting edge of society in impacting communities for Christ. We know that He has so designed it, that His Church is the hope of the world because She carries the message of the Savior. So, we want to be one of thousands and tens of thousands of churches that represent Him well and are a wholesome expression of the character and nature of the Risen Christ.

We sense in so many ways that our church is just getting off the ground. We just celebrated 20 years of ministry, and we're just becoming an adult. If we stay humble and broken and dependent upon Him so He is free to move by His Spirit as He wills, there is no limit to what can happen in the years to come. We pray the same thing is true in the local church that you are a part of.

In the fall of 2003, Christ The Rock had the unique privilege of giving birth to a daughter church. CTRCC Green Bay has been launched and is growing. What a joy to see my youngest brother, Jim, sense a direct calling on his life from God to pastor a church. He has stepped over his fears and in faith and courage has given himself over to the challenging, yet absolutely thrilling, privilege of being an under-shepherd in His Church.

Chapter 12

REFLECTIONS ON
MY PARENTS

One of the greatest joys in my life was seeing both my mother and my father come to know Jesus personally and to watch them grow in their relationship with Him. I remember quite distinctly the day we were at our cottage for a church picnic. There were about 50 people there, and we had planned a water baptism. Fifteen freshly-redeemed people stood in the water that day to publicly identify with the death, burial, and resurrection of Christ through water baptism.

My mother was one of those 15. She shared her testimony and made such a clear and powerful profession of her faith in Christ that day before she went under in the waters of baptism. My father didn't object but saw no need for it. He was quite reserved and quiet about his faith. After my mother's baptism, you couldn't keep her quiet about her Savior. She could strike up a conversation with anybody and was always able to turn it to include sharing about Jesus in a warm, delightful, loving, non-offensive way. She was contagious.

Several years later, we were up at the cottage again for a church picnic with over 100 people. When it was time for the baptism, many sat on our dock and the neighbors' dock that extended by those in the water into a big circle. My brother, Bob, and I were doing the baptism. We had baptized about 30 people and asked if there was anyone else. We waited a few minutes and no one was coming. Then, Bob noticed our dad coming from the shoreline onto the dock. We whispered to each other that he was probably coming out to check the boat. He walked past the boat. We surmised he was going to check something on the end of the pier. He got to the end of the dock, sat down, slowly lowered himself into the water, and started to walk towards us. We whispered quickly to each other, "He's coming out here. What do you suppose he's doing?"

He came and stood in front of us, looked us both in the eyes and said, "I want to be baptized; would you baptize me?"

Neither of us could believe it. We both had tears running down our cheeks. He turned and faced everyone and declared openly and non-apologetically his sincere faith in Jesus Christ and his desire to be baptized as a symbol of his identification with the death, burial, and resurrection of Jesus from the dead.

As we all were standing there, listening to him, my eyes glanced at the dock, the boat, the cottage, and then out across that lake. In that moment, my mind flashed pictures and memories from throughout the years, like a 30-second TV infomercial. With the backdrop of thousands of great memories at this place, with this exceptional man I called Dad, was a moment that would top them all.

This little lot on Lake Poygan was a getaway place all my life. It was the place I spent thousands of hours out in a boat with my father. It was a place of all of our family vacations. It was a place of campfires and marshmallows on a stick. It was a place of croquet and horseshoes, of cookouts and barbecues. It was a place of sitting in lawn chairs and telling stories and laughing at jokes. It was a place of cleaning fish and frying them up. It was a place of a lot of work, and even more fun; of water-skiing and body-surfing, of catching toads and diving for clams, of fixing broken boat ramps and watching storms race across the lake.

It was the place that God had orchestrated for me to meet His Son on September 5, 1975. And here we were, standing in the water, surrounded by our church family, and my father is humbling himself and asking his two sons-turned-preachers to baptize him. That event is like the star on the top of a Christmas tree. There are literally thousands of wonderful, warm, delightful memories with my dad at that cottage, but this one sits on top of them all.

HARD TO SAY GOODBYE

My parents became very active in our church. They would rarely miss the weekly early morning prayer meetings on Wednesdays. They were so supportive of me and my brothers in our pursuit of ministry.

In early March 1999, the doctors had to remove my mother's gallbladder. Tests discovered a cancer. They had hoped that the cancer was contained in the bladder, but worried that it wasn't because of a hole in the lining of the bladder. There was a high chance it had leaked out, and they recommended chemotherapy and radiation treatments. It was so hard to see the effects of the treatments on her.

My father was retired and took care of her, hand and foot, during this whole time.

After four months, they had determined that she was cancer-free. We were all elated. She was still weak but gradually was gaining her strength back. By mid July, we were all suspicious because she just wasn't herself, and the recovery wasn't what it was supposed to be. Upon testing, they found cancer had come back with a vengeance.

We had about a week with her around her hospital bed. Her pain was minimal and even on her deathbed, she kept giving . . . serving . . . loving others. She motioned to each of her daughters-in-law, one by one, to come near to her. She spoke words of life and powerful encouragement to each of them.

She did the same with her sons and with her daughter. I'll never forget the words she spoke to me that day. She again asked for forgiveness for the ways she had failed me and hurt me through

138

the years. She affirmed me as her son, as a man, as a husband and father, as a leader, as a pastor, as a preacher, as a son of God.

A younger couple from the church, who my mom was friends with, had just had a baby. They brought the newborn with them to visit her on one of her final days. When she saw the baby, she was so overjoyed for them. She asked to hold this tiny, new little girl. When they handed the baby to her, she lifted the baby up and began to pray and dedicate this newborn to God and to His purposes. The couple, along with myself and other family members present, couldn't hold back the tears. It was a tender, powerful moment as what typified her life was also being demonstrated in her dying.

She was a servant. She was weak and in pain and a few days from death, and she was thinking of others. She is giving of her heart to minister to whoever came into her room. For that is how she lived; and is how she lived as she was dying. Oh, her spirit of others-centered loving would be more prevalent in the lives of Christ-followers today.

In her final days, she was conscious and could still communicate. On Thursday, I asked her if she was ready to be with Jesus. She said, "Oh, yes, in three more days." On Friday, she said, "Oh, yes, in two more days."

Doctors didn't know for sure, so I decided I would still preach at our services that weekend. I went up to see her after our Saturday night service. I reminded her I loved her. Sunday morning we had three services. Two were on our main campus, and one was held in between the other two services at an off-campus location in a theatre. The off-site service began at 9:30 a.m. I would usually get up to preach around 10:10 a.m. and be finished by 10:45 a.m. so that I could get back in time to preach at the service that began at our main campus at 10:30 a.m. With my father, my brother, Bob, and our family physician by her side, my mother left this earth to be with Jesus on Sunday, August

8, 1999, at exactly 10:30 a.m. I think this is no coincidence. At 10:30 a.m., I was in the middle of preaching at one of our services, while the worship was beginning at another one of our services. She went into His very presence at a moment in time when her oldest son was doing what she loved to do so much – singing praises to our God and King. The timing was impeccable.

When I arrived at the main site to preach at that service, I was told that my mother had died. I left immediately to go to the hospital. They ended up sharing with everyone that my mom had died and played a video of my message that had been recorded from the earlier service.

On my way to the hospital, the song that was playing in my car was "Redeemer, Savior, Friend." The words that stand out to me are,

> *I know You had me on Your mind the day You climbed upon that hill. And You looked at me with eternal eyes, while I was yet in sin . .*

. Redeemer, Savior, Friend. Redeemer, change my heart again. Savior, come and rescue me from sin. You're familiar with my weakness, devoted to the end. Redeemer, Savior, Friend.

I wept so hard as I worshipped. I worshiped the Lamb of God for rescuing me from sin, and my mom, and my whole family. I knew without a doubt that my mother was in God's very presence at that very moment, and though the loss was so great, the realization that Christ had saved her and redeemed her, and that she was with Him was overwhelming. Through my tears and groaning, I was worshipping our Redeemer, our Savior, our Friend.

A TRIP OF A LIFETIME
NO REGRETS

A week after Mom died, we had a scheduled fishing trip to Canada with Dad, my two brothers, Bob and Jim, and me. About a year and a half earlier, Bob was talking to Dad one day and asked him if he had any regrets in his life. Dad thought for a few moments and said, "Not really. Well, I wish I would have come to know Jesus earlier than I did – that's about it." Then, he hemmed and hawed a little and said, "Well, I always wanted to go to Canada, fishing, but it's no big deal."

Bob called me later that day and told me of the conversation and said, "Let's book a trip."

So, we talked to Jim and had booked a fly-in fishing trip to Canada for the week of August 14-21. The trip had been scheduled for almost a year.

So, here we were – at the funeral on Tuesday night, August 10, wondering if we should still go.

One of the sons said, "Dad, what do you think Mom would want us to do, go or not?"

He said, "Definitely, go." So that clinched it. We decided to go.

It proved to be a great way to allow us to be together and grieve together the loss of this incredible woman. There were four of us, and each day we'd rotate who we would fish with that day. So all day, each day, for seven days, each of us three sons got to spend an entire day alone with Dad in the boat.

The discussions we all shared with each other were so powerful and so healing. We laughed, we cried, we reminisced and told stories; and we caught boatloads of fish – something we all enjoy doing. It was a week divinely ordained and orchestrated by the Hand of our Loving Father. Little did we know how much time we would have left with him.

It was September 8, 2000. It was a warm, sunny Friday, and the day of our annual men's retreat. I had gone up north a few days early with a couple of friends to go musky fishing. The plan was to go to the men's retreat directly from our fishing trip.

144

We had a great time and Friday, after lunch and some cleanup, Curt, John and I headed towards Silver Birch Ranch in northern Wisconsin.

The retreat was slated to begin at 6:30 p.m. that evening. We were about to turn off the main highway onto the road leading to the camp, when we were waved down by a men's ministry leader and friend. He looked serious. I rolled my window down and he said, "Bill, I'm sorry to be the one to tell you this, but your dad had a heart attack."

I questioned, "Are you sure? Are you sure he didn't just have a seizure?" No, it was a heart attack, and the ambulance came to take him to the hospital in Antigo, about 25 miles from the camp. "Is he okay?"

"I'm not sure. They were working on him . . ."

I was shocked. I couldn't believe what I was hearing. We immediately headed off to the hospital. I begged with God not to let this be the time. I kept whispering to God, "I'm not ready to say goodbye to my dad. . . I'm not ready."

We didn't talk much as we drove. What was there to say? I tried to call my two brothers. Bob was in Virginia, speaking, and couldn't be reached. I did get through to Jim, who lives in Green Bay. I told him I'd call him from the hospital.

When we arrived, there were several guys from the church standing outside trying to console me. One showed me where I needed to go. I was led into the room, and no one else was there. My father's motionless body was lying still on a stretcher. His wallet, clothes, and other personal items were lying on the table. I lost it. I felt grief so deep inside of me that I never remember ever feeling before. I sobbed and kept saying, "No, not yet. No, I'm not ready to say goodbye. Dad, I can't say goodbye. I'm not ready."

I laid my head on his chest, and held him, and wept. I held his hand in mine and looked intently at his hands. I reminisced about all those hands had done for me. How many times those hands had hugged me, wiped tears from my eyes, put worms on a hook for me, or written notes of encouragement to me. Those hands went to work every day to provide for our family. Those hands pointed direction, brought loving discipline, and patted me on the back. For 43 years those hands guided me, served me, loved me well-- but not anymore. As he lay there, I thought of the words, "He is not here, he is risen."

It was exactly 13 months to the day since my mom had left for Heaven, and now he was joining her. It was only one day after what would have been their 46th wedding anniversary. It was only three days after I celebrated my 25th spiritual re-birthday.

Early that morning, my father, along with two of his church friends, Dick Hietpas and Jim Nelessen, left early to go up to the men's retreat. They stopped for lunch on the way up. They set up Dick's camper when they arrived. Then they played a couple of games of cribbage. The two other guys were going to go for a walk, and my dad decided to take his daily 15-minute nap. When they returned, he was gone. It appeared he had awakened and began to sit up. As he did, he had a massive sudden heart attack and fell back into the bed. One of the guys at the retreat was a doctor and tried to resuscitate him but to no avail. Suddenly and abruptly, he had left one world and entered into another.

A couple of verses that have given me great comfort and strength; I Corinthians 15:26, which says,

> *The last enemy that will be abolished is death.*
> *There will be no more enemies for the believer;*
> *after death, home free.*

I Corinthians 15 also assures of the resurrection of the dead for all who believe.

The other verse is I Thessalonians 4:13-14:

> *That you may not grieve as do the rest who have no hope. For if we believe that Jesus died and rose again, even so God will bring with him those who have fallen asleep in Jesus.*

It has been so difficult to say goodbye to my mom and dad. I often wonder, "What are they doing this moment in Heaven." I anxiously await with great longing and expectation to see them again when I cross that Great River.

Chapter 13

WHAT NOW, WHAT NEXT?

As I write this, it is early May 2004. I confess the unique challenges of leadership in a growing church. I keep assuming that someday it's going to get easier, but it doesn't. There is much pressure, responsibility, criticism, and difficulty in leadership. But I can't think of anything I would rather do, and give my life to, than being a part of The Church that Jesus promised He would build and that the gates of hell would never prevail against (Matthew 16:18). I also confess that the heartaches and challenges are used to continue to reduce me to new levels of deeper dependence upon The Living God.

151

I want to be a part of a prevailing Church that wants to flesh out who Jesus is, in how we treat each other, and in how we reach out to a lost and dying world all around us. None of us knows how long we have left on this earth. I want every day to count in making a difference for eternity. I want to be a part of an alive, healthy, vibrant, active, grace-giving, love-motivated Church that is Spirit-led, Christ-centered, and God-honoring.

I want to be a part of a Body that sees all of life as an opportunity to glorify God and worship Him; that not only believes the Word of God, but wants to live it; that wants to be a living, loving expression of Christ on the earth; that is moving away from self-centered living to other-centered living; a people who are an answer to Jesus' prayer that we would be one, as He and The Father are One, and that subsequently the world will know that the Father had sent Jesus (John 17:21); that we are genuinely loving each other the way that Jesus loves us (John 13:34-35) and the world will know we are Jesus-followers — because of how we love each other (John 13:35); a community that is honest and genuine, who doesn't pretend and act like we have it all together, when we still really struggle; who are grace-givers – because we've been grace-receivers; that doesn't escape from painful realities or run from conflicts with others, but who in humility face reality and address conflicts with the hope of restoration and resolve; who have the courage to face a fallen, sin-stricken world, as well as the personal struggles within, with hope and grace that only the gospel offers.

A Church that believes in the value of every part of the Body and releases people to serve Christ, according to His calling, and how He has gifted them; a fellowship of believers who are passionately pursuing God and who are genuinely desiring to live out Christian community in how we love and relate to each other; a Church that pursues unity, yet celebrates diversity; a Body that isn't just inward and preoccupied but has a vision for the lost; that vision includes a neighbor, a coworker, a relative, a friend, but it also includes a heart for other cities and other nations. A Church that is going into all the world to make disciples, teaching them to observe all things – whatever He has commanded.

ON A PERSONAL NOTE

I must tell you, I am so honored to be pastor of the group of people called Christ The Rock Community Church. They are family. They have a heart for God and a genuine love for people. The leaders are godly men and women who want their lives to count, for Jesus' sake.

Janet is the director of our mission department and oversees all of our cross-cultural ministries. She is known as the mother of the Saharawi people because of her years of involvement with a special people group of refugees, who now live in the Sahara Desert in Algeria but who were from Western Sahara. Thirty years ago, they were driven out of their homeland, and now as a people, live in tents in the Algerian Sahara Desert, 180,000 plus.

Our three sons are each devoted Christ-followers and have a heart to serve God.

Basically, I want to end by saying,

> *This one life will soon be past.*
> *Only what is done in Christ will last.*

I often pray a prayer that Jonathan Edwards was noted as praying –

> *Lord, stamp eternity on my eyeballs.*

> *For what shall it profit a man if he gains the whole world and loses his soul. Matt 16:26*

> *For our life is a vapor that appears for a short time, then vanishes away (James 4:14).*

Lord, make me to know my end and what is the extent of my days. Let me know how transient I am. Behold, You have made my days as handbreadths and my lifetime as nothing in Your sight. Surely every man at his best is a mere breath (Psalm 39:4-5).

I want to grow as a loving,
Christ-like husband and father.
I want to mature as a servant-leader, in
reflecting Christ as a pastor-leader.
I want to reach out to the world around
me with hope and help in Jesus' Name.
I want the rest of my life to count for eternity.

Lord,
by Your Grace and for Your Great Name,
let it be so.

Christ The Rock Menasha WI
December 5, 2017 · 🌐

With heavy hearts, we must share some devastating news. Our beloved Senior Pastor, Bill Lenz, passed away on the afternoon of December 4 ,2017.

Bill had been suffering from depression for the last three months. He was seeing a counselor and doctor and reaching out to friends for help in walking through this, but depression eventually claimed his life on earth.

But that is not his legacy. We remember him as a man with an immense heart for the lost and the hurting, who loved God and lived to serve Him and others. Bill brought the hope of Jesus Christ to thousands of people during more than 35 years of ministry.

In light of those truths about Pastor Bill, it is unbearably difficult to comprehend how he could lose sight of hope himself. We are left with many questions and deep sorrow for our dear pastor, leader, brother and friend.

Please pray for his family and our church family.

FACEBOOK ANNOUNCEMENT 12/5/2017

Lenz, William C.

William (Bill) Cary Lenz left us unexpectedly on Monday, December 4, 2017, at the age of 60. He was living in Tustin, in his lifelong dream home on the lake.

Born on June 10, 1957, at St. Elizabeth Hospital in Appleton, Wisconsin, Bill was raised in Little Chute by David and Janice Lenz with sister, Lois, brothers Robert (Bob), James, and Timothy (Timmer). He attended Elementary, Middle and High Schools in Little Chute. He was active in football, lots of drug-doing and trouble-making throughout his high school years. Incredibly, Bill came to faith in Jesus Christ at age 18, thanks to a Billy Graham TV broadcast he chanced upon watching at the Lenz family cottage. He was never the same again. Following high school, Bill enlisted in the United States Coast Guard where he served our country and began his study of the Scriptures. After his four years in the Coast Guard, he attended a Bible College at World Challenge in Tyler, Texas. Then he became a youth group leader at Evangel Church in Menasha while working at WEMI radio station.

There he met the love of his life, Janet [Gregg] Lenz. They were married on February 27, 1981. Wasting no time, together they started Solid Rock Ministries, and a year later founded the present-day Christ The Rock Community Church. He tirelessly gave himself to this church for the past 35 years.

He is survived by his wife, Janet, three sons: Ben (Jessie); Nate (Jenny); and Seth (Kate); grandchildren Michiah, Hadessa, William, Everett, Ezekiel, Moses, Eva, Theodore, Jedidiah, Lucille, and Thaddeus. He is also survived by an incredible extended family who loved this man dearly, and were loved well by him. He leaves behind a church body and staff at Christ The Rock that will miss him beyond what words can express. He is preceded in death by his parents, David & Janice Lenz; brother, Joey Lenz (at birth); brother, Timmer Lenz; and a wealth of people who are forever in eternity with Jesus because of his life's work and calling.

Bill was an avid fisherman, hunter, devoted husband, proud father, an in-love opa (grandfather), and lover of nature. Most of all, he was a fisher of men. You'd be hard-pressed to spend more than a few hours with him without Bill pulling out his Bible to spend some time with his Lord & Savior. He was our family's living "Bible Concordance" before our smartphones offered such amenities. He served on the Executive Board of the National Association of Evangelicals for nine years. He also served on the board for World Relief for a number of years. His work reached to Romania, India, Sierra Leone, Rwanda, Israel, Haiti, Algeria, and remote bush villages in Alaska. His reach was worldwide and eternal, following his motto "let eternity be stamped on my eyeballs" perfectly. He couldn't even officiate a wedding without sharing the Good News of Jesus. He had a passion and love for peoples' hearts--desiring to see them tap into their own stories to find healing and hope in Christ. This passion led to the establishment of Character Development, a study course that has grown to become a truly life-changing class.

Bill had an undeniable love for Jesus, and an unstoppable love for the world. Wherever he went, he shared from his heart the Hope of Christ. Even throughout these days of funeral preparation, his wife and sons encountered countless people who tearfully expressed how their own lives had been impacted by him, whether business people, clerks, funeral and cemetery personnel, bankers...and on and on.

Bill has never fallen victim to depression in the past, but has battled it with a vengeance for the last 3 months. He sought and accepted help, but unfortunately for all of us, it wasn't enough to give us more time with him here on earth. Our hope in Jesus Christ is the same today as it was before this nightmare began. Please, if you're struggling with depression, don't go at it alone. Seek help.

There will be a visitation from 1:00 p.m.-5:00 p.m. at Christ The Rock Church in Menasha on Sunday, December 10, 2017, immediately followed by a worship service celebrating Bill's life at 5:00 p.m. Military Honors will follow the service with the Neenah/Menasha Veterans Honor Guard assisting.

INSIGHTS FROM A
FELLOW SHEPHERD

Reading these amazing stories of God's power and grace in Bill's life and ministry, we wouldn't be human if we didn't struggle in reconciling his extraordinary life and his tragic death. The whole explanation is known only to God, but I'd like to share my perspective.

A little after five o'clock on Thanksgiving morning in 2017 my phone rang. A pastor friend in Cincinnati was on the other end. "Mark, I'm sorry to call you so early on Thanksgiving, but I have a pastor friend in Wisconsin, a great man of God, a gifted leader, who's been going through something like you experienced. I think it would mean a lot if you could talk to him and share your story. I assured him I would, and he gave me Bill's contact information.

A few minutes later, I got another call. This man introduced himself as Crawford Lipsey, a very close friend of Bill's, and he wanted me to have more background information before I talked with Bill. The more he told me Bill's story the more it mirrored my own. An hour later, my phone rang again, and this time it was Bill.

Maybe before I talk about that call, I should tell you, even though I'd never met Bill, why I wound up talking to him that morning.

Something happened to me eight years ago, that I could have never dreamed possible. Without warning, during the most productive season of my life, with everything looking wonderful to people on the outside, with no apparent reason, I just broke down. Here's a little of my story.

I came to my church in 1985. As a Texan, I could have never imagined spending my life and ministry in Kansas, but next year I'll be at NewSpring for 34 years, and it's been the ride of a lifetime. But there were so many seasons of challenge. I use that word euphemistically. The church I came had about 350 people, it was entrenched in legalism and rigidity, and frankly, the changes I made had to be implemented slowly. They were also painful.

But over the next twenty years, I did what I could. And God blessed. We grew to 600 in attendance, and in 1991 I began looking for land to relocate. That began an eight-year process to relocate. It was impossible for 7 years and fifty-one weeks! But God did a miracle. We moved in to our new campus in 1999 with a property worth ten million dollars that we paid three hundred thousand dollars for. As you can imagine, God actually did many miracles.

By 2004, we had grown to 1,200 in attendance, had a thriving regional television ministry, but I realized we were primarily reaching the already convinced. I woke up one day and thought to myself, if this is what ministry is, I don't think I want to keep doing it. I began asking the question, what would I do to be effective in reaching the spiritually unresolved if I had no fear of upsetting those who are here?

That began a four-year season of transition that was the hardest time in my life. As we made the transitions to be effective, many people were unhappy. Add to that, Wichita was changing dramatically. Industries and companies that had been rock solid were either drying up or leaving the area. Between the people who left angry, and those who moved away for employment reasons, over a four-year period, we lost 800 of the 1,200 who attended. But strangely enough, we never dropped below 1,200 in attendance. Even though many left, the unchurched and unsaved were streaming in our doors. God was dramatically changing lives, and this was what I'd always dreamed of experiencing as a pastor.

For several years, attendance grew by almost a thousand people a year. It was thrilling, but it was a challenging season. By the beginning of 2010, attendance had jumped to nearly 4000, great numbers of people were coming to Christ every week, and our median age had dropped from the mid-forties to the late twenties. The conflicts were basically resolved. In a way, it felt like paradise.

I probably should have recognized the storm clouds building on the horizon. I lost two key staff members that I really loved and counted on. I couldn't complain. They were going to greater callings, but the pain of their loss and wondering how I was going to replace them was tough. Then my father-in-law who I'd been close to, died suddenly. And if I'd been paying attention, I'd have recognized that, although things were great at the church, the weight of the previous years had taken their toll.

On November 27th of 2010, I left the church campus after preaching the second Saturday service, and headed home. Somewhere between church and my house, something just snapped. I didn't see it coming, had no warning it was coming, never experienced it before, and most of all, had no idea what it was. Emotionally I just collapsed. For the next several months, I became a person I didn't know. I'd always been the one in charge that people depended on, and suddenly, I couldn't do simple things. Like driving. I conflated simple aches and pains to the assurance that I was dying. And then, since I was sure I was dying, I jumped to the conclusion that I'd done something to fail God, and now He was punishing me. There aren't words to say what a deep, dark hole I descended into for a couple of months. Only the grace of God and my wife who never left my side, got me through.

Someone might ask, what about mental health care? Eventually it was a great resource, but whatever I dealt with was hard to identify since it seemed, for several reasons, to fly in the face of usual diagnoses. Worst of all, I think I know

now, what people refer to when they talk about "celebrity medicine." Several of the mental health professionals I encountered at first, awkwardly treated me as a megachurch pastor. I just wanted to be treated like any ordinary person. Thankfully, in time, I got that help.

By mid-January, I was able to return to a semi-normal life. When I came home, I had a choice to make. I could either sugarcoat my story as to why I'd had to take time off, or I could share the gut level painful, candid story of the darkness I fell into. I chose the latter, and when I shared my story, I was amazed how my phone would ring constantly over the last eight years with both church and corporate leaders saying that they were going through a very similar thing.

And that's how I wound up talking to Bill that Thanksgiving morning.

As he told me what he was feeling, it sounded so similar to my own experience. Knowing that it might not be the same thing I went through, I asked if I could share my story with him. For the first twenty minutes or so, I could hear hope rising in his voice. Suddenly, I heard the optimism dissipate as he returned to the fear that God was finished with him. At that point, I asked him to consider flying with his wife out to Wichita. I assured him that they could stay with us, and that we would take care of them. His response haunts me to this day. He said, "That sounds great, but I don't think I could get through the airport." My mind raced back to a cold December morning in 2010 when it required every ounce of energy I had to make it through our small airport.

For all who wonder how a man who lived such an extraordinary and effective life for Christ, could finish his race down here in such a sad way, I'm here to tell you that I do understand. I've been there. Frankly, if I'd never gone through that dark valley, I might not believe it possible, but now I know.

Within a couple of days of Bill's death, Christian media outlets attempted to write about Bill's life and death. I couldn't shake the sense that some of the things I read were off target. Knowing that Bill's friend, Crawford Lipsey was going to be spending a lot of time with the family, I reached out and shared my feelings with him in a text. This is what I wrote.

Crawford, my friend,

I keep thinking about Bill. Just read a news item about him in (a Christian media source), and I'm chilled by how similar our experiences were. Beyond that, it's hard to realize how far off people are from understanding. This goes beyond depression or anxiety.

It defies psychological and psychiatric profiles. After going through it myself and listening to others, none of us seems to understand how it started, what it was, or what exactly brought us out. What is standing out to me, is a kind of personal that's profile is forming in my head:
* Pastor of a mega church or major ministry
* Usually in 50's or '60's.

* A strong leader.

* But remains vulnerable, "touchable."

* Tries to be as available as he was when ministry was smaller .

* It's a season of change, especially staffing key position(s).

* (key) The onset of whatever this is, started with some kind of sudden physical symptom that makes the leader feel that ministry may be over. Which morphs into the idea that God is through with us.

* These guys all have a strong purity in their lives. Not the kind who cheat on their wives or behave unethically. They humbly feel their own sinfulness, and constantly wonder why God chose them.

* From that point we go into a free fall as we invent a whole new, totally dark reality, which almost no one can penetrate.

And when people try to help us, nothing works primarily for 2 reasons:

1. People want to tell us how great we've been, but we tend to believe our failure is between us and God. And because our thinking is skewed, we can only find the verses that speak on judgment. And since we've spent our lives in the Book, believe me, we know where they are.

2. We know all the counseling techniques, we've used them, ourselves, and again, because our thinking is skewed, we just foul them off.

Sorry to be so long, it's just that I know, as a friend, you will have a voice to speak into the lives of many who are grieving. They need to understand; this is not your "garden variety" depression or anxiety disorder. The professionals don't quite have a handle on this yet. Since it's episodic in nature and not chronic, the pros would have to reanalyze some of their definitions of disorders.

As a hunter, you know there are different calibers and loads designed to bring down different game. I'm convinced, whatever this is, it's Satan's load to bring down big game.

Thanks for your patience, Crawford. I had to get this off my heart.

Blessings, my friend,
Mark

In closing, I don't know than any of us who've gone through such a valley, or those who love us and stand by, will ever completely understand. Perhaps the best explanation is simply remember that we are flawed, imperfect humans, loved and called by the perfect God, who knowing our weaknesses, loves and uses us anyway. The Psalmist said it best, I think in the 103rd Psalm.

11 For his unfailing love toward those who fear him is as great as the height of the heavens above the earth. 12 He has removed our sins as far from us as the east is from the west. 13 The Lord is like a father to his children, tender and compassionate to those who fear him. 14 For he knows how weak we are; he remembers we are only dust.
Ps 103:11-14NLT

Mark Hoover
NewSpring Church
Wichita, Kansas

LOVE NOTES
FROM JANET

The first time Bill Lenz crashed into my world was a Sunday night at the church we both attended. I was the sign language interpreter that night, and with my back to the speaker, I began translating what was being said. The speaker was a new guy I had not yet met, a Coast Guard sailor, who was telling his story of God's Divine Interruption of his life. His passion for God seemed to exude from his very pores. About half-way through, I turned from my chair to see this young man whose story I was relaying to the deaf group in front of me.

I remembered thinking, "Whoever this guy is, I hope that if he ever gets his head out of the clouds and lowers his dreams of being like Paul (including remaining *single*), I hoped that he'd somehow see me."

He did, and our first date was listening to his sermon on *Grace*....being preached to me sitting all alone in the auditorium as the only listener. It was passionate, sincere, and rather long. But I knew that if he'd ever considered having a wife by his side, I'd gladly be first in line.

Less than a year later, we returned from our honeymoon and Bill began his official street ministry … full-time, no income, a little borrowed office in the Salvation Army building, and a passion for the Good News that had already drawn a growing group of un-churched young adults whose lives had been eternally altered by Bill's pursuit, love, and contagious faith. He worked full-time, and we survived on $425/month - with a new baby on the way. None of it made any sense, other than a deep conviction in our hearts that there was a very lost world at our doorstep, waiting to hear about Jesus.

The outreach grew, expanding beyond the downtown streets and into schools and a 24-hour Life-line.

We began a Friday night gathering time for all those who were seeking and beginning new lives as followers of Jesus. Under strong encouragement from some very Godly men in our lives, we prayerfully began meeting on Sunday mornings, as a Church. There was a wonderfully refreshing atmosphere in those gatherings, as so many people who had found new lives. Jesus' Spirit living inside them brought Hope and Life to so many who had never known it before.

As the church grew, we moved from building to building to accommodate the growing numbers of Believers coming through the doors.

Our family grew as well....with 3 young boys bringing great joy and love into our home. Bill loved taking them hunting, fishing, hiking, camping...all the things that were wonderful memories from his own childhood. He was a skilled fisherman.

And he was a passionate *Fisher of Men.*

We tried to put boundaries around our family, but the ever-growing needs of the church often touched our home life. Our boys grew up knowing a life that included the strangers who often joined us around the table, and the church entity - our 4th Child - was simply a part of our family's life. The boys grew with awareness of the needs of others, and developed hearts of compassion, tenderness, and at times, sacrifice. There was lots of love, laughter, and closeness. Bill and I talked frequently about them together, knowing the risks of pastor's kids getting lost amidst the demands of ministry. We considered them a part of what we were doing, and they grew into loving young men, husbands and fathers. We often talked about how very, very grateful and proud we were of our sons.

The pressures of leading a large church were always there, but Bill fought giving into the disappointments, exhaustion, insecurities and criticism that comes with the senior pastor role.

He never spoke of giving up or walking away. His love for God and people never waned, even though the cost of full-time leadership ministry is great.

Bill loved people. He had lived his first 18 years without the Hope that comes into a heart and life through living in a personal relationship with God, and he was passionate to point people to God. He was passionate for people to find Hope and Purpose and Value through Jesus. We couldn't go anywhere that he wouldn't find someone to meet and talk to. (His boyish energy came out most often, like whenever he saw a shopping cart in a parking lot. He simply had to hop on it and ride through the lot...always looking for someone to call out to with a warm greeting.)

Bill was my greatest cheerleader, strongest support, loving companion, wise advisor, compassionate listener, and closest friend. He loved me so well! He listened to my perspective on the things happening in our lives, our boys, the church, . . . everything. Though there was often push-back in our discussions, he would give more consideration and we usually ended up coming to a shared agreement and respect together. I never, ever doubted his love for me. *He loved me so very well.*

He will always remain in my mind and heart as that passionate man who knew what it was like to be lost and without hope when he was without Jesus, and he was committed to bringing the Hope he had found in Christ to a lost world….whether in his small hometown, or to the Fox Valley, or to other places in the world….even to refugees living in a desert on another side of the world. High energy, quick to laugh, a huge heart for "crippled" humanity, and a passionate love for people…. He was an avid Fisher of Men, always seeking after the Fisher of Men who had captured his heart.

Our family had the incredible privilege of his big presence in our lives...in our home...in our thoughts and hearts. He loved well. SO very well.

INSIGHTS FROM A SON

From Ben, the oldest and wisest son. And oldest.
Did I mention oldest?

As I have walked through a year of not having
my dad, I've realized just how much of a part of
my life he is, and how much I miss him. No day
passes without me thinking about him. I can see
his influence on my life at every turn.

As a kid, I loved how involved he was with me and
my brothers. We would regularly be fishing in a
boat, tubing or skiing. We hiked in the woods, we
camped in the wilderness, we threw the football in
the backyard. I treasure the time I had with him.

As I grew up, he stayed involved in my life, and cared very much for our family. He would write out scriptures on a white index card and give them to us before school. Though he had much waiting for him at the office, he prioritized time with us, even in the short car rides to drop us off at school. I miss that time with him.

Fishing. Oh gosh, the fishing with dad was one of my favorite times with him. He taught me how to slay the Northerns, run a boat, and invite people into that sacred space. I seriously appreciate how much he brought us fishing and the time spent in the boat enjoying sunsets, cruising on the water, and talking about anything on our minds. It's funny how many of my fond memories are in a boat with him.

I'm grateful he taught me how to hunt too. Hunting was a fun activity, but the real driver was time together. It was the drive together, texting each other throughout the hunt, and celebrating a success that was so meaningful. I treasure my memories of our many hunts together, the guy time with dad, my uncles and brothers, and how safe I felt when he was around. I miss calling him on my way home from the woods, or him being the first I call when I shoot something. One of my first hunts as a teen, I shot a deer and in my excitement I yelled from my stand, "Dad! Dad! . . . Dad?" after 3 minutes, I finally heard, "What?" Oops, I totally screwed up the rest of his hunt that day, but he answered me through the quiet woods. Then he came to help me with my deer. He cared for me. Deeply. And I know this.

Preaching. At first, I kind of roll my eyes because I've heard all of his stories (so many times), and I could probably tell you his main points for any subject. But I've come to appreciate this more and more. He was such a man of conviction. He couldn't sit still when he felt there was a message from God to be spoken. Dad was that way behind closed doors too. At home, away from the spotlight, he believed everything he preached. He practiced his sermons on me before they were sermons :)

Seriously though, he was a walking concordance. From as young as I can remember, I would just randomly ask dad, "Dad where is this phrase in the Bible?" and he would nail the verse reference. He had a reference for anything, and often would quote the bible even when we were just hanging out and joking around.

I loved how he would often fall asleep with the bible tipped on his chest, with a highlighter hanging out of his mouth, dog tired.

I admire his love for lost people. He was strong, bold, and sometimes even over-confident, but he was also tender hearted, fun, and he loved well. He stayed engaged in relationship when others would quit. He tried to work things through, even when it was rough. He always called when there was tension between us, and he apologized a lot. Man, that's so rare in our day… a father who apologizes, regularly. He felt things so deeply, right to his bones. So when he felt bad, he felt bad head to toe. And when he offered love, it was from all of him. When he felt passionate, oh boy he felt it with every fiber in him. His hands would shake when he was preaching, not from nerves but from conviction.

And this isn't to ignore his weaknesses, in fact his weaknesses were not very easy to hide. He would get defensive at times, insecure, even fearful. But in his weakness, he would talk about what was going on. He would ask for help. He modeled a leader who was open about his faults and let Jesus keep working on him. That was remarkable. I still can't totally reconcile how such a driven, passionate leader would so regularly use himself as the example of how God was changing a life from darkness to light. Never perfect, never claimed to be, but honest about the struggle of life. I miss that too, a lot.

He gave his life to others, for the sake of knowing Jesus. His life was so radically changed when he met Jesus, he just had to keep telling others about Him. I'm so thankful he did. My life is forever changed because I also now know the undeserved grace God poured out on my life through Jesus. I have no other hope than that of the saving power of Jesus. My efforts to be a good man fell woefully short the first day I started trying. I cling to the righteousness that was freely given to me, not based on anything I've done to earn it, but as a generous gift from a loving Dad.

Sure, dad fell short in many ways of modeling the pure love and life of our heavenly Father. But he got the best things right, foremost of all – showing me grace through Jesus.

See, I don't feel this is all lost. I carry this all forward with me, ingrained into who I am. His life is not marked by the dreadful loss to depression or the way he died, but how he lived his life only by grace. It's not just a catchy phrase he signed his letters with, he embodied that truth.

I miss my dad a ton. I grieve the fact that new memories will be paused while I continue on this earth, but he's helped shape me into who I am today. I'd be thrilled and honored if I were to become half the man he was. Not height-wise, we already got gipped out of the tall genes.

Thank you for taking the time to read, I feel it's a way that we all can somehow continue to grieve, appreciate and love the man for who he was. Our family has been supported by countless notes, calls, meals, prayers and conversations. Thank you, sincerely.

I know if he were writing this, he would want all glory for anything good he contributed to be redirected to Jesus.

Then he would have one more point before praying to close the service.

Then one more point after the last song.

Miss you dad,

Ben

Isaiah 40:28-31

Do you not know? Have you not heard?
The Everlasting God, the Lord, the
Creator of the ends of the earth
Does not become weary or tired.
His understanding is inscrutable.

He gives strength to the weary,
And to him who lacks might He increases power.

Though youths grow weary and tired,
And vigorous young men stumble badly,

Yet those who wait for the Lord
Will gain new strength;
They will mount up with wings like eagles,
They will run and not get tired,
They will walk and not become weary.

Hebrews 12:1-3

Therefore, since we have so great a cloud of witnesses surrounding us, let us also lay aside every encumbrance and the sin which so easily entangles us, and let us run with endurance the race that is set before us, fixing our eyes on Jesus, the author and perfecter of faith, who for the joy set before Him endured the cross, despising the shame, and has sat down at the right hand of the throne of God.

For consider Him who has endured such hostility by sinners against Himself, so that you will not grow weary and lose heart.

Stay Connected!

Stay connected and informed of future
books planned from the writing and
sermons of Pastor Bill Lenz.

www.pastorbilllenz.com